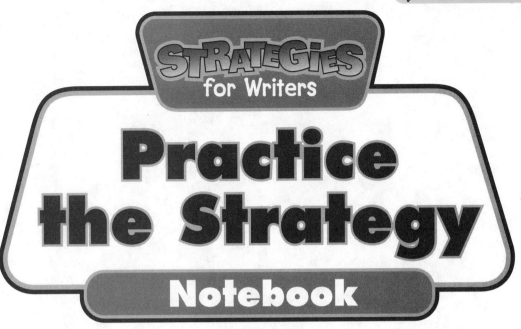

STRATEGIES for Writers

Practice the Strategy

Notebook

Level G

Authors

Leslie W. Crawford, Ed.D.
Georgia College & State University

Rebecca Bowers Sipe, Ed.D.
Eastern Michigan University

Cover Design
Tommaso Design Group

Production by Marilyn Rodgers Bahney Paselsky

Literature Permission
p107, Hornik, Susan B., "For Some, Pain Is Orange." *Smithsonian*, February 2001,
p 48. Permission granted by Susan B. Hornik, freelance writer and editor.

ISBN 0-7367-1249-6

Zaner-Bloser, Inc., P.O. Box 16764, Columbus, Ohio 43216-6764   (1-800-421-3018)

Printed in the United States of America

04 05 06   MZ   5 4 3

Table of Contents

NARRATIVE writing

EXPOSITORY writing

Table of Contents

DESCRIPTIVE writing

PERSUASIVE writing

Table of Contents

EXPOSITORY writing

TEST writing

Prewriting

Gather
List things my audience should know about my topic.

The notes below are about a 4-H Club honey-making project. These notes will help the writer to write a personal narrative about her experience.

honey-making exhibit for 4-H Club

always nervous about projects for County Fair

watched PBS special about beekeeping, got interested

love honey

started project in spring

harvested in August, just in time for County Fair

4-H specialist for Natural Resources, Mr. Macono, helped me

ordered bees and hives

nervous about getting stung

honorable mention from judges

beekeeping and honey-making information:

    safety equipment

    hive and combs

    sweeping bees away from combs

    removing wax from cells

    removing honey from combs

    straining and purifying honey

Prewriting

Gather
List things my audience should know about my topic.

your own writing

Now it's your turn to practice this strategy with a different topic. Think of an experience that you'd like to write about. Make notes about what your audience will need to know about your experience. Include notes about

- the event itself—what happened, when and where it happened, why it happened, and who was involved (the 5 W's).

- any information that you think will help your audience understand your story.

Notes

_____

_____

_____

_____

_____

_____

_____

_____

_____

_____

_____

_____

_____

_____

RETURN Now go back to Tony's work on page 21 in the Student Edition.

Prewriting

Organize Make a 5 W's chart to organize my notes.

The beekeeper used her notes on page 6 of this notebook to fill in the categories in the 5 W's chart.

What happened?

- bought hives and bees, raised bees, made honey
- exhibited my work at County Fair
- won honorable mention

Who was there?

- me, Mr. Macono, my parents, the judges

Why did it happen?

- always nervous about projects for County Fair
- watched PBS special about beekeeping, got interested
- love honey

When did it happen?

- started project in spring
- harvested in August, just in time for County Fair

Where did it happen?

- County Fair

Prewriting

Organize Make a 5 W's chart to organize my notes.

your own writing

Now it's time for you to practice this strategy. Using the notes you made on page 7 of this notebook, fill in the categories in the 5 W's chart. Make sure you have enough details for all categories. Add more notes if you need to.

What happened?
Who was there?
Why did it happen?
When did it happen?
Where did it happen?

RETURN Now go back to Tony's paper on page 22 in the Student Edition.

Write

Draft my narrative. Start with a lead paragraph that presents the 5 W's in such an interesting way that the audience will want to read more.

There are many kinds of lead paragraphs you can write. Tony's lead paragraph included the 5 W's, and it also introduced the event and explained its importance. Here is a lead paragraph for the honey-making paper that follows this pattern. (The paragraph contains some errors. You will get a chance to correct them later.)

I allways used to get nervous when County Fair time came along. Most of my friends in 4-H were raising animals to exibit, but I don't live on a farm. Last winter, I watched a PBS special on beekeeping. Decided that would be my project this year. With the help of my adviser, Mr. Macono, I not only set up hives and extracted honey from them. I even won honorable mention at the fair!

Discussion: Was this a good lead paragraph? Why or why not? Would you have written it differently? If so, write how you would have done it.

_____

_____

_____

_____

_____

_____

_____

_____

_____

Narrative Writing • *Personal Narrative*

Drafting

Write
Draft my narrative. Start with a lead paragraph that presents the 5 W's in such an interesting way that the audience will want to read more.

your own writing

Now it's time for you to practice this strategy. Write your own lead paragraph. Include as many of the 5 W's as you can. Follow one of these patterns:

- Build the lead paragraph around a **quote or saying**.
- Build the lead paragraph around a **dramatic fact**.
- Build the lead paragraph around a **character**.

_____

_____

_____

_____

_____

_____

_____

_____

_____

_____

_____

_____

_____

Now go back to Tony's work on page 24 in the Student Edition.

11

Revising

Elaborate
Check each paragraph for supporting details.
Make sure they relate to the topic sentence.

Now it's your turn to practice this strategy. For the rest of this chapter, you will work with a personal narrative written by the beekeeper. Four sentences below could be supporting details for a paragraph about how nervous she was when getting ready to handle the bees. Write the four sentences that you think could be supporting details under the topic sentence below.

Supporting details:

Reminding myself about the beekeeping program on TV was a big help.

The equipment cost a bit of money, but Mr. Macono helped me raise the cash.

I was so excited about my honey-making project that I could almost taste the honey before I ever worked with the bees.

I practiced moving slowly so that I would not disturb the bees too much.

Until then, I had never realized how much fun beekeeping could be.

I started by trying to get comfortable with the equipment.

I remembered how uncomfortable my new bicycle helmet was the first few times I wore it.

Finally, I was ready to go in and work.

Topic Sentence: It took a while to build up my courage to actually handle the bees.

_____

_____

_____

_____

_____

_____

_____

_____

ReVising

Elaborate
Check each paragraph for supporting details. Make sure they relate to the topic sentence.

Now it's time for you to practice this strategy. Here are details that need a topic sentence. Write a topic sentence for each paragraph.

_____

_____

_____

You can buy hives with or without bees in them. I decided to purchase hives with bees, for I thought this would be easier for a beginner like me to handle. I made my choices and placed my orders in January.

_____

_____

_____

I was still awkward in the vest, veil, and big gloves. I was also still a little scared. The thought of bees crawling all over me was unsettling. The gloves were difficult to work in and I felt like I was moving in slow motion. Still, I knew I had to start sometime. I took a deep breath and stepped up to the hive.

Remember: Use this strategy in **your own writing**

 Now go back to Tony's paper on page 25 in the Student Edition.

ReVising

Clarify

Make sure sentences and paragraphs are in the most effective order.

Now it's time for you to practice this strategy. The sentences below make up a paragraph about how the writer extracted the honey from the hive. Number the sentences in what you think is the most effective order. (Hint: The notes on page 6 may help you.) Then copy the sentences in the order you assigned.

_____ With the wax gone, it was a fairly easy job to extract the bees' precious product.

_____ I did this by sweeping the bees away from the comb with a bee brush.

_____ When I first started trying to move them, the bees got a little agitated, so I used the bee smoker to calm them.

_____ I began the job by getting the bees away from the honeycomb.

_____ Once I separated the bees from the comb, I used a knife to remove the wax covering from each cell.

_____ Seeing all that beautiful golden honey, the fruit of my (and the bees') labors, was a great thrill.

_____

_____

_____

_____

_____

_____

_____

_____

_____

_____

Remember: Use this strategy in **your own writing**

 Now go back to Tony's work on page 26 in the Student Edition.

Narrative Writing • Personal Narrative

┐ Indent.
≡ Make a capital.
/ Make a small letter.
∧ Add something.

ℓ Take out something.
⊙ Add a period.
New paragraph
SP Spelling error

Editing

Proofread

Check to see that there are no sentence fragments or run-on sentences.

Now it's time for you to practice this strategy. Here are the first three paragraphs of the personal narrative about raising bees. Use the proofreading marks to correct any errors. Use a dictionary to help with the spelling.

I allways used to get nervous when County Fair time came along. Most of my friends in 4-H were raising animals to exibit, but I don't live on a farm. Last winter, I watched a PBS special on beekeeping. Decided that would be my project this year. With the help of my adviser, Mr. Macono, I not only set up hives and extracted honey from them. I even won honorable mention at the fair!

My first step was bying hives and bees. You can by hives with or without bees in them. I decided to purchase hives with bees, I thought this would be easier for a beginner like me to handle. I made my choices and placed my orders in january. That way, I would be sure to get my Equipment by early spring. Around the time honey making began.

It took a while to build up my courage to actually handle the bees. I started by trying to get comfortabel with the Equipment. I put on my vest and then took my veil out of its pouch. I attached the veil to a wide-brimmed hat that I had, following the instructions that came with the veil. I told myself that yes, bees would be crawling allover me. I practiced moving slowly so that I would not disturb the bees too much. I kept reminding myself about the beekeeping program on TV I was so fasinated by it. Finally, I was ready to go in and work.

Remember:
Use this strategy in
your own writing

Now go back to Tony's work on page 28 in the Student Edition.

Using a Rubric

Use this rubric to evaluate Tony's essay on pages 29–31 of your Student Edition. You can work with a partner.

Audience

How effectively does the writer present the 5 W's *(who, what, when, where, why)* in the introductory or lead paragraph?

Organization

How well does the writer organize events and information that the reader needs to know?

Elaboration

How consistently do the writer's paragraphs have a clear focus and/or a topic sentence with strong supporting details?

Clarification

How well does the writer present details in an order that makes sense?

Conventions & Skills

How well does the writer avoid fragments, run-ons, and sentence punctuation errors?

your own writing

Save this rubric. Use it to check your own writing.

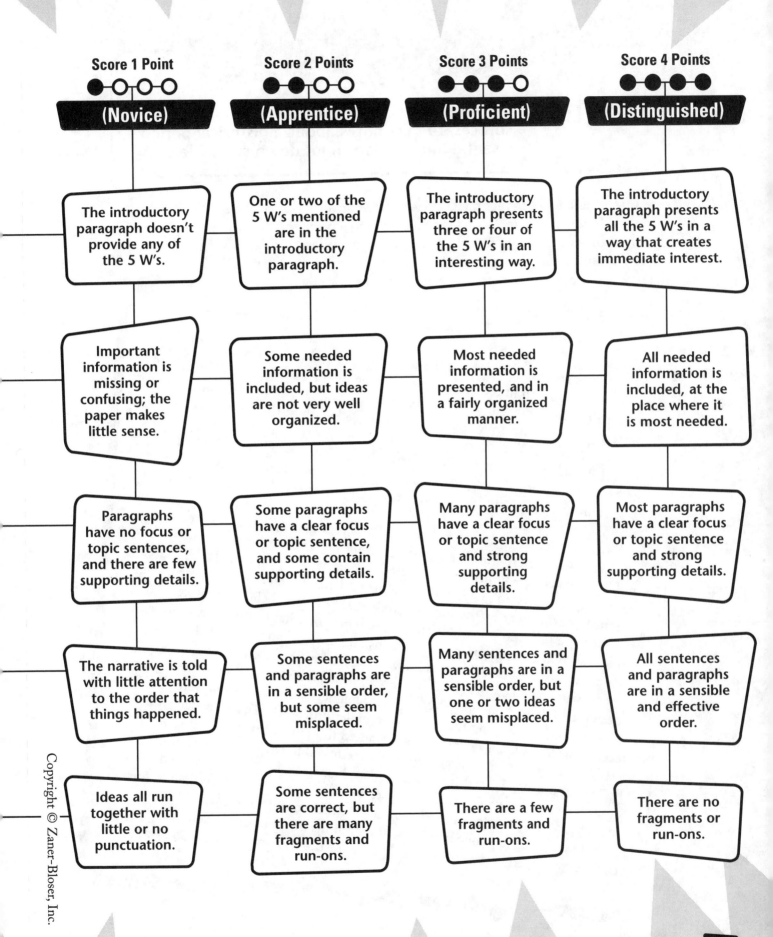

Score 1 Point

(Novice)

The introductory paragraph doesn't provide any of the 5 W's.

Important information is missing or confusing; the paper makes little sense.

Paragraphs have no focus or topic sentences, and there are few supporting details.

The narrative is told with little attention to the order that things happened.

Ideas all run together with little or no punctuation.

Score 2 Points

(Apprentice)

One or two of the 5 W's mentioned are in the introductory paragraph.

Some needed information is included, but ideas are not very well organized.

Some paragraphs have a clear focus or topic sentence, and some contain supporting details.

Some sentences and paragraphs are in a sensible order, but some seem misplaced.

Some sentences are correct, but there are many fragments and run-ons.

Score 3 Points

(Proficient)

The introductory paragraph presents three or four of the 5 W's in an interesting way.

Most needed information is presented, and in a fairly organized manner.

Many paragraphs have a clear focus or topic sentence and strong supporting details.

Many sentences and paragraphs are in a sensible order, but one or two ideas seem misplaced.

There are a few fragments and run-ons.

Score 4 Points

(Distinguished)

The introductory paragraph presents all the 5 W's in a way that creates immediate interest.

All needed information is included, at the place where it is most needed.

Most paragraphs have a clear focus or topic sentence and strong supporting details.

All sentences and paragraphs are in a sensible and effective order.

There are no fragments or run-ons.

Prewriting

Gather
Use several references, including primary sources, to take notes about a historical period. Use the information to jot down story ideas.

Suppose that, after a lot of thought, you decide that your story will be about the time that Rome burned, in A.D. 64. You have found a primary source, a description of the event by a writer called Tacitus, on the Internet. Read what Tacitus says about the fire. (Important place names are in italics.) Then read the glossary of place names that comes after his description.

. . . Now started the most terrible and destructive fire which Rome had ever experienced. It began in *the Circus*, where it adjoins the *Palatine and Caelian hills*. Breaking out in shops selling inflammable goods, and fanned by the wind, the conflagration instantly grew and swept the whole length of the Circus. There were no walled mansions or temples, or any other obstructions, which could arrest it. First, the fire swept violently over the level spaces. Then it climbed the hills—but returned to ravage the lower ground again. It outstripped every counter-measure. The ancient city's narrow winding streets and irregular blocks encouraged its progress.

Terrified, shrieking women, helpless old and young, people intent on their own safety, people unselfishly supporting invalids or waiting for them, fugitives and lingerers alike—all heightened the confusion. When people looked back, menacing flames sprang up before them or outflanked them. When they escaped to a neighboring quarter, the fire followed—even districts believed remote proved to be involved. Finally, with no idea where or what to flee, they crowded on to the country roads, or lay in the fields. Some who had lost everything—even their food for the day—could have escaped, but preferred to die. So did others, who had failed to rescue their loved ones. Nobody dared fight the flames. Attempts to do so were prevented by menacing gangs. Torches, too, were openly thrown in, by men crying that they acted under orders. Perhaps they had received orders. Or they may just have wanted to plunder unhampered.

[The emperor] Nero was at *Antium*. He returned to the city only when the fire was approaching [his] mansion. . . . The flames could not be prevented from overwhelming the whole of the Palatine, including his palace. Nevertheless, for the relief of the homeless, fugitive masses he threw open the *Field of Mars*, including Agrippa's public buildings, and even his own Gardens. Nero also constructed emergency accommodation for the destitute multitude. Food was

Prewriting

Gather
Use several references, including primary sources, to take notes about a historical period. Use the information to jot down story ideas.

brought from *Ostia* and neighboring towns. . . . Yet these measures, for all their popular character, earned no gratitude. For a rumor had spread that, while the city was burning, Nero had gone on his private stage and . . . had sung. . . .

Glossary of place names in Tacitus' Story

the Circus, an enormous stadium for horse races and other shows. Its full name was Circus Maximus.

the Palatine and Caelian hills, two of the seven hills that Rome was built on

the Field of Mars, an open area with some buildings for the public

Ostia, a town about 20 miles from Rome

Antium, one of Nero's palaces

your own writing

Now it's your turn to practice this strategy. Use the material you just read to make notes for a story set at the time of Rome's burning.

_____

_____

_____

_____

_____

_____

["The Burning of Rome, 64 AD," EyeWitness—history through the eyes of those who lived it, www.ibiscom.com (1999).]

 Now go back to Quiana's work on page 44 in the Student Edition.

PreWriting

Organize   Make a story map to organize my ideas.

Now it's time for you to practice this strategy. Choose an incident in the eye-witness account to build a historical fiction episode. Begin to plan out your story. Use information from your notes, as well as your own ideas about other events to include.

Setting:
Where: Rome
When: A.D. 64

Major Characters:

Minor Characters:

Plot/Problem:

Event 1:   **Event 2:**   **Event 3:**

Outcome:

 Now go back to Quiana's work on page 46 in the Student Edition.

Use after page 49 in the Student Edition.

Drafting

Write
Draft my story. Make sure it flows smoothly from beginning to middle to end.

Now it's time for you to practice this strategy. Here is the opening of a historical fiction episode about the fire in Rome. Read the paragraphs, and then do the activity that follows them. (The paragraphs contain some errors. You will get a chance to correct them later.)

A Witness to the Great Fire

Perdicus was a harness maker, and his son, Marcellus, was his apprentice. They lived in Ostia, only about 20 miles from Rome, but they rarely made the trip there. This time they had to deliver an order. Perdicus had a big order to supply riders in a race at Circus Maximus.

"help me pack the wagon, Marcellus, Perdicus said. We will leave in the morning."

Marcellus did not have to be asked twice. The journey would be hard, but he had never been to rome. He told himself "that this would be the most exciting trip of his life."

They arrived in Rome late in the day. Marcellus' aunt and uncel, with whom they would be staying, lived close to the Circus Maximus.

Read the list that follows. To make the rest of the story tie together and flow smoothly, which five items should be included? Mark each one with an X.

____ a discussion of the games Marcellus played with his cousins
____ a description of the crowded streets near the Circus Maximus
____ a description of the many temples throughout the city
____ an explanation of how Marcellus' father made harnesses
____ Marcellus' eyewitness account of how the fire started
____ a description of how the fire spread
____ an explanation of how the horse races were organized
____ an explanation of how Marcellus helped his relatives escape
____ a conclusion telling why this was the most exciting, but frightening, trip of Marcellus' life

Drafting

Write
Draft my story. Make sure it flows smoothly from beginning to middle to end.

your own writing

Use your notes from the story map on page 20 to draft your episode.

_____

_____

_____

_____

_____

_____

_____

_____

_____

_____

_____

_____

_____

_____

_____

_____

_____

_____

 Now go back to Quiana's work on page 50 in the Student Edition.

Narrative Writing • Historical Fiction Episode

ReVising

Elaborate
Add historical details to make the story authentic.

Now it's time for you to practice this strategy. Here are four historical details that could be added to the story. Add at least three of them in the places where you think they work best. Reword the details to make them fit into the story. (The paragraphs contain some errors. You will get a chance to correct them later.)

- Streets in the area near Circus Maximus were narrow and winding.
- Merchants transporting goods to Rome could only bring their wagons through the streets at night.
- Many people in Rome kept dogs as pets.
- Stores sold a variety of good products, such as fine linen tunics.

They arrived in Rome late in the day. Marcellus' aunt and uncel, with whom they would be staying, lived close to the Circus Maximus.

The next morning, Marcellus amused himself by walking through the streets with his cusin and looking into the stores. He was enjoying the sweet aromas from the bakeries and the perfume sellers when he noticed a strange smell.

"Is that not the odor of burning cloth," he said to Terence?

"I do believe you are correct," Terence replied. "It would be advantageous for us to warn the others".

They turned and ran back toward Terence's family's apartment. Allready there was thick smoke filling up the whole neighborhood.

Remember: Use this strategy in *your own writing*

Now go back to Quiana's work on page 51 in the Student Edition.

ReVising

Clarify   Make sure dialogue sounds realistic.

Now it's time for you to practice this strategy. Here are some lines of dialogue that might be used in a story about Rome's burning. Rewrite each one so that it sounds more like real speech. (Use a dictionary if you need help with any of the words.)

1. "I feel a great deal of concern about this excessive heat and wind," said Marcellus' aunt.

   _____

   _____

2. "It is imperative that you depart from the city immediately!" shouted the soldier.

   _____

   _____

3. "How shall I ever determine the most effective route of departure?" cried the old woman.

   _____

   _____

4. "The summit of that edifice shall soon come careening into the thoroughfare," Marcellus shouted.

   _____

   _____

5. "There are vast multitudes of people congregating in the Field of Mars," Marcellus' father reported.

   _____

   _____

6. "Why has not our esteemed emperor aided us in our time of woe?" one citizen wondered.

   _____

   _____

Remember: Use this strategy in **your own writing**

Now go back to Quiana's work on page 52 in the Student Edition.

Narrative Writing • Historical Fiction Episode

Indent.

Make a capital.

Make a small letter.

Add something.

Take out something.

Add a period.

New paragraph

Spelling error

Editing
Proofread
Check to see that quotations are punctuated correctly.

Now it's time for you to practice this strategy. Here are the first several paragraphs of this historical fiction story about Rome. Use the proofreading marks to correct any errors. Use a dictionary to help with spelling.

A Witness to the Great Fire

Perdicus was a harness maker, and his son, Marcellus, was his apprentice. They lived in Ostia, only about 20 miles from Rome, but they rarely made the trip there, as robbers often lay in wait for travelers along the road. This time they had to go. Perdicus had a big order to supply riders in a race at Circus Maximus.

"help me pack the wagon, Marcellus, Perdicus said. We will leave in the morning."

Marcellus did not have to be asked twice. The journey would be hard, but he had never been to rome. He told himself "that this would be the most exciting trip of his life."

They arrived in Rome late in the day. Marcellus' aunt and uncel, with whom they would be staying, lived close to the Circus Maximus. That night Perdicus and Marcellus would bring their wagon into the city and unload it at the Circus.

The next morning, Marcellus amused myself by walking through the streets with his cusin and his dog and looking into the stores. Some shops specialized in beautiful linen tunics, better quality than Marcellus had ever seen at home. He was enjoying the sweet aromas from the bakeries and the perfume sellers when he noticed a strange smell.

"Is that not the odor of burning cloth," he said to Terence?

"I do believe you are correct," Terence replied. "It would be advantageous for us to warn the others".

They turned and ran back toward Terence's family's apartment. The streets in this area were narrow and winding. Allready there was thick smoke filling up the whole neighborhood.

Now go back to Quiana's work on page 54 in the Student Edition.

Using a Rubric

Use this rubric to evaluate Quiana's essay on pages 55–57 of your Student Edition. You can work with a partner.

Audience

How well does the writer hold the audience's interest throughout the story?

Organization

How clearly does the story flow from beginning to middle to end?

Elaboration

How effectively does the writer use historical details to make the story sound authentic?

Clarification

How realistic is the dialogue spoken by the characters?

Conventions & Skills

How consistently does the writer use the correct punctuation for quotations?

your own writing

Save this rubric. Use it to check your own writing.

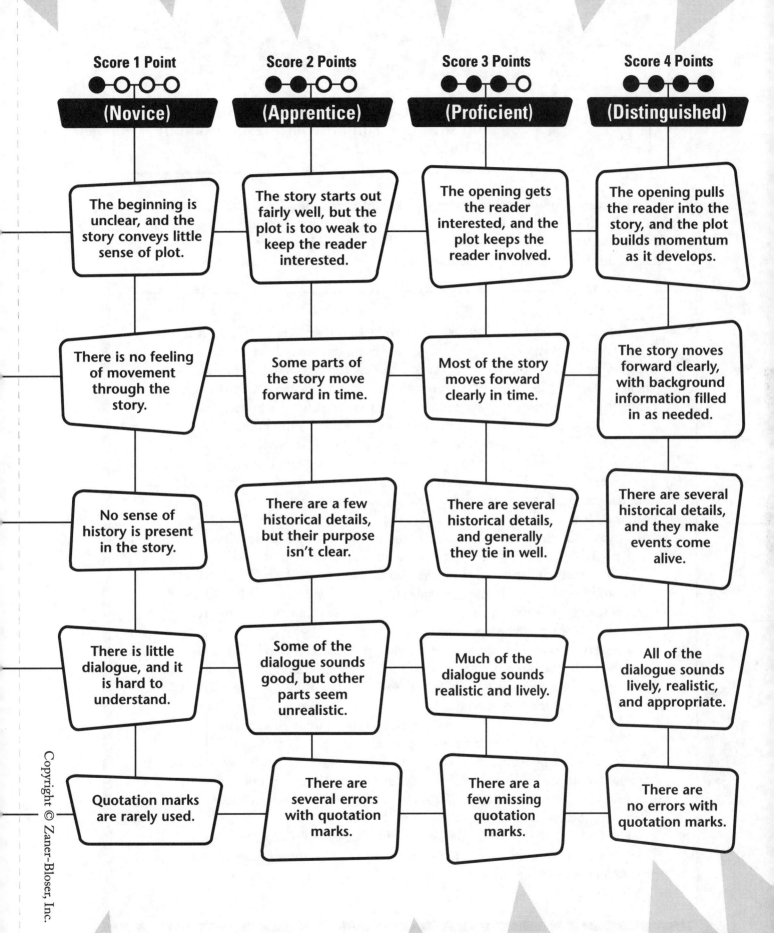

Score 1 Point ● ○ ○ ○ (Novice)

The beginning is unclear, and the story conveys little sense of plot.

There is no feeling of movement through the story.

No sense of history is present in the story.

There is little dialogue, and it is hard to understand.

Quotation marks are rarely used.

Score 2 Points ● ● ○ ○ (Apprentice)

The story starts out fairly well, but the plot is too weak to keep the reader interested.

Some parts of the story move forward in time.

There are a few historical details, but their purpose isn't clear.

Some of the dialogue sounds good, but other parts seem unrealistic.

There are several errors with quotation marks.

Score 3 Points ● ● ● ○ (Proficient)

The opening gets the reader interested, and the plot keeps the reader involved.

Most of the story moves forward clearly in time.

There are several historical details, and generally they tie in well.

Much of the dialogue sounds realistic and lively.

There are a few missing quotation marks.

Score 4 Points ● ● ● ● (Distinguished)

The opening pulls the reader into the story, and the plot builds momentum as it develops.

The story moves forward clearly, with background information filled in as needed.

There are several historical details, and they make events come alive.

All of the dialogue sounds lively, realistic, and appropriate.

There are no errors with quotation marks.

Prewriting

Gather

Use an Internet search engine to find credible Web sites that can answer questions about my hobby or interest.

Now it's your turn to practice this strategy with a different topic. Suppose that you are interested in the house of the future—what it will look like, what new devices and features it will have, and so on. To get some perspective on the topic, read this article about five "future" homes that were built in 1933.

Not many outsiders visit the small town of Beverly Shores, Indiana. It is off the main highway, along Lake Michigan. But hidden away here are five remaining houses from the Century of Progress Exposition, a World's Fair held in Chicago in 1933–1934. All of the houses were located on the Fair's "Street of Tomorrow," a showcase for housing designs for the future.

The house that got the most attention at the Fair was the House of Tomorrow. This house was three stories high and had twelve sides, with walls made of glass. Some people thought it looked like a wedding cake. This house was one of the first to have such conveniences as an automatic dishwasher, an electric garage door opener, and central air conditioning. Besides a garage for a car, the House of Tomorrow had a garage for an airplane. (For a long time designers believed that every family would own a plane—at least a helicopter.) The house was also way ahead of its time in that it was solar heated.

Another remaining house from the Fair is the Cypress Log Cabin. All the walls and floors of this house are made of cypress wood. Essentially a chalet-shaped cabin, it boasts an electric stove that has a permanent cooking well or pot inside it. The one bedroom has several levels for sleeping.

The Armco-Ferro House was built out of prefabricated steel. The steel was covered with baked porcelain enamel. One of the house's original features was kitchen cabinets that were hung on the walls. (Before this, most people had movable cupboards.) Steel houses such as the Armco-Ferro were built in many areas after World War II. They were designed for middle-class families.

The Wieboldt-Rostone House was the least successful of the five. The Rostone Company built it to show off its new siding material. It was a manufactured stone called Rostone. However, this material did not hold up to the weather. It was replaced in the 1950s by a material called Permastone. Permastone also fell apart.

The fifth house is the Florida Tropical House. It had one of the earliest two-story living rooms. Inside the living room is an aluminum staircase that led to an overhanging balcony.

Prewriting

Gather
Use an Internet search engine to find credible Web sites that can answer questions about my hobby or interest.

Here are some topics related to houses of the future that you may want to find more about. For each topic, rate the Internet sources in terms of how reliable they sound. Mark the best **a,** the second-best **b,** and the third-best **c.** Then write a short explanation of why you selected **a** as you did.

1. **the family room in the house of the future**

   _____ a site run by the American Society of Home Designers that includes models and diagrams of present and future family rooms

   _____ a site describing what movie stars want in their family rooms

   _____ a site of future family rooms drawn by architecture students

   _____

2. **the totally automatic house**

   _____ a site run by an electrician who is building such a house

   _____ a site with a story by Ray Bradbury called "There Will Come Soft Rains," which involves a completely automatic house

   _____ a site run by the Electronics Group of America, with a section on the topic "Are We Ready to Build Automated Houses?"

   _____

3. **building materials for the house of the future**

   _____ a site run by an inventor who has created a new construction material

   _____ a site describing building materials, with comments from builders

   _____ a site run by a large city newspaper, with an article discussing the advantages and disadvantages of new synthetic building materials

   _____

4. **past ideas for houses of the future, and how well they worked**

   _____ a site featuring "The World's Fair Houses: Wisdom or Folly?"

   _____ a site with photos and comments by someone who owned such a house

   _____ a site run by the American Society of Future Dreamers

   _____

Remember: Use this strategy in *your own writing*

 Now go back to Charlotte's work on page 69 in the Student Edition.

Prewriting

Organize

List, in order of importance, three questions to ask the Web site about my topic.

your own writing

Now it's time for you to practice this strategy. Imagine you have found a Web site called *futurehomes.org*, which deals with all aspects of "houses of the future," including those designed in earlier times. Write notes for three questions that you would ask the question-and-answer column of this Web site. Follow this procedure:

* Review the article and the list of topics on the previous two pages to get ideas for possible questions. (Or use ideas of your own.)

* Choose questions that lead to a discussion. Avoid questions that require only a yes or no answer.

* Decide which question is most important to you and why you think it is important. List that question first.

Order-of-Importance Organizer

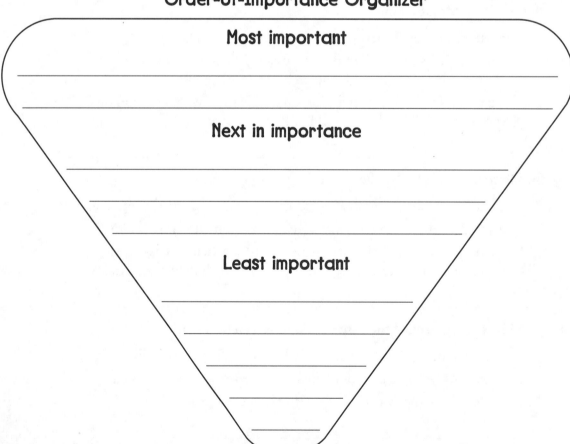

Most important

Next in importance

Least important

RETURN
Now go back to Charlotte's work on page 70 in the Student Edition.

Drafting

Write
Draft the body of my e-mail. Put my questions into a clear format.

Now it's time for you to practice this strategy. Use the notes in your order-of-importance organizer to write your three questions to *futurehomes.org*. Use this structure to draft the body of your e-mail:

- Put each question into a short paragraph. Put the question at or near the beginning of the paragraph.
- Use the rest of the paragraph to give background or an explanation of why you are asking the question.
- Number your questions.

Use this page and the next for your work.

| Address | |
| Subject | |

Drafting

Write — Draft the body of my e-mail. Put my questions into a clear format.

 Now go back to Charlotte's work on page 72 in the Student Edition.

ReVising

Elaborate

Check that my tone is appropriate and that my introduction and conclusion fulfill their purpose.

Now it's time for you to practice this strategy. Here is the final section of an e-mail that one writer sent to *futurehomes.org*. Revise the section. Correct any problems with tone, and reword the final paragraph to make it clear that the writer wants an answer. You will work with the introduction of this e-mail in the next activitiy.

3. The house of the future—that's really where it's at. The Century of Progress Exposition in 1933 had a bunch of them. Tell me what they had at other world's fairs.

I think people's ideas about future houses are pretty interesting.

_____

_____

_____

_____

_____

_____

_____

_____

Remember: Use this strategy in *your own writing*

 Now go back to Charlotte's work on page 74 in the Student Edition.

ReVising

Clarify Make sure that I have observed good e-mail etiquette.

Now it's time for you to practice this strategy. Here is the beginning of one writer's e-mail to *futurehomes.org*. Revise it to correct any errors in e-mail etiquette. (The paragraphs contain some other errors. You can correct them now or later.)

Address	futurehomes.com/quest
Subject	an interest of mine

Date: Thurs, 27 June 2002

From: mwattlem@surprise.net

   I live in a pretty old house that has only a few up-to-date features. For instance, we FINALLY got a dishwasher last year. :-) I've did a little research into futuristic houses and would be grateful if you culd answer a few questions.

   1. What kinds of things could we have in future kitchens? I know some people have microwaves and trash compactors now. It would be GREAT to hear about any devises that might make my life easier someday.

Remember: Use this strategy in **your own writing**

RETURN Now go back to Charlotte's work on page 76 in the Student Edition.

Editing

Proofread

Check the e-mail address. Be sure that past and past participle verb forms are used correctly.

⊐ Indent.	ℓ Take out something.
≡ Make a capital.	⊙ Add a period.
/ Make a small letter.	# New paragraph
∧ Add something.	⑤ℙ Spelling error

Now it's time for you to practice this strategy. Here is the e-mail to *futurehomes.org*. Use the proofreading marks to correct any errors. Use a dictionary to help with spelling.

Address | futurehomes.com/quest

Subject | questions about future houses

Date: Thurs, 27 June 2002

From: mwattlem@surprise.net

I live in a pretty old house that has only a few up-to-date features. For instance, we finally got a dishwasher last year. I've did a little research into futuristic houses and would be grateful if you culd answer a few questions.

1. What kinds of things could we have in future kitchens? I know some people have microwaves and trash compactors now. It would be great to hear about any devises that might make my life easier someday.

2. People have wrote stories about totally automatic houses. Recently I seen articles on vacums that run themselves. What other ideas do inventors have?

3. I know at least five homes of the future were built for the Centery of Progress in 1933. What other fairs have shown new housing ideas?

I'd apreciate any information you could give me to answer my questions.

Max Wattleman

mwattlem@surprise.net

Remember: Use this strategy in **your own writing**

Now go back to Charlotte's work on page 78 in the Student Edition.

Using a Rubric

Use this rubric to evaluate Charlotte's e-mail on page 79 in the Student Edition. You can work with a partner.

Audience

How clearly and politely does the writer communicate with the audience (the reader of the e-mail)?

Organization

How effectively has the writer used order of importance in organizing questions or comments?

Elaboration

How well has the writer explained the purpose of the e-mail in the introduction and the importance of getting an answer to it in the conclusion?

Clarification

How well does the writer observe good e-mail etiquette?

Conventions & Skills

How accurately does the writer use past and past participle forms of verbs?

your own writing

Save this rubric. Use it to check your own writing.

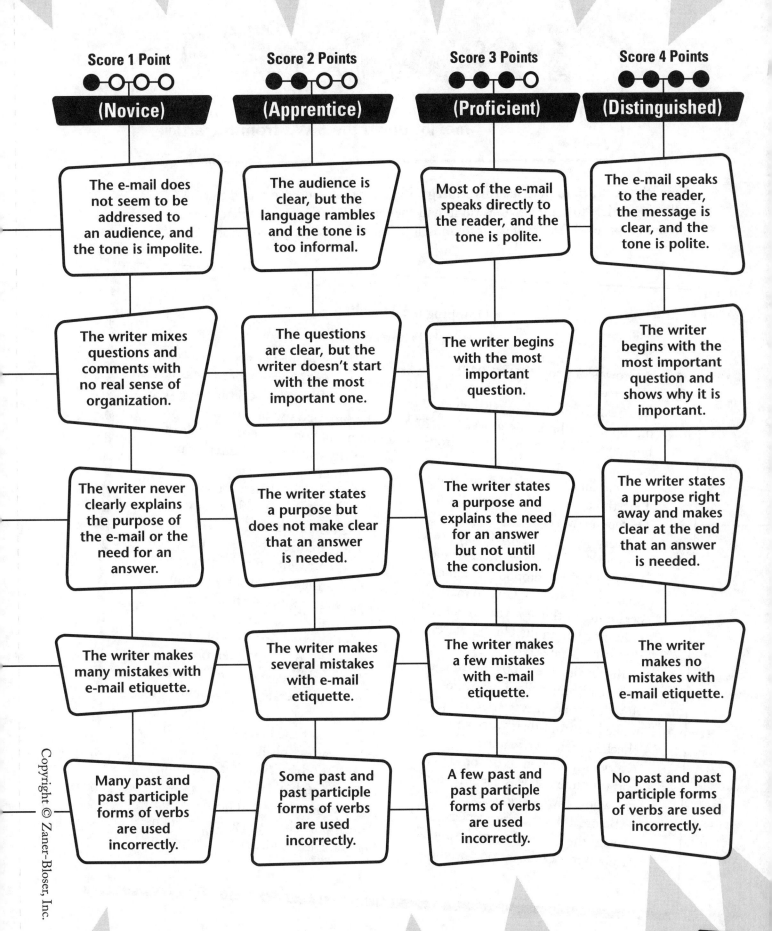

Score 1 Point
●─○─○─○
(Novice)

Score 2 Points
●─●─○─○
(Apprentice)

Score 3 Points
●─●─●─○
(Proficient)

Score 4 Points
●─●─●─●
(Distinguished)

The e-mail does not seem to be addressed to an audience, and the tone is impolite.

The audience is clear, but the language rambles and the tone is too informal.

Most of the e-mail speaks directly to the reader, and the tone is polite.

The e-mail speaks to the reader, the message is clear, and the tone is polite.

The writer mixes questions and comments with no real sense of organization.

The questions are clear, but the writer doesn't start with the most important one.

The writer begins with the most important question.

The writer begins with the most important question and shows why it is important.

The writer never clearly explains the purpose of the e-mail or the need for an answer.

The writer states a purpose but does not make clear that an answer is needed.

The writer states a purpose and explains the need for an answer but not until the conclusion.

The writer states a purpose right away and makes clear at the end that an answer is needed.

The writer makes many mistakes with e-mail etiquette.

The writer makes several mistakes with e-mail etiquette.

The writer makes a few mistakes with e-mail etiquette.

The writer makes no mistakes with e-mail etiquette.

Many past and past participle forms of verbs are used incorrectly.

Some past and past participle forms of verbs are used incorrectly.

A few past and past participle forms of verbs are used incorrectly.

No past and past participle forms of verbs are used incorrectly.

Prewriting

Gather
Read an article on a topic that interests me. Jot down the 5 W's from the article.

Now it's your turn to practice this strategy. Let's say that you have found the following article to summarize. Read it, and then complete the activity that follows on page 40. You may want to underline important points as you read.

Dropping the Time Ball

by Pamela D. Greenwood

Crowds of people shiver on the cold city streets. Some check their watches. Others look up at the ball on top of a tall mast on a nearby building. Finally the ball starts dropping and a chant begins.

"Ten, nine, eight, seven, six, five, four, three, two, one." People cheer! "Happy New Year!"

Every year since 1907 (except twice during World War II—in 1943 and 1944), a ball has dropped in Times Square in New York City to mark the beginning of the new year. It is the only time ball in the United States that still operates.

But in the late 1800s most major cities had time balls. They were dropped at noon every day. People looked up from their work and checked their own watches. Everybody wanted to be "on time," and the time ball was a signal that the whole town could see.

Before 1883 there was no standard time in the United States. A sundial or noon mark (a mark on a windowsill that the sun reached at noon) helped people tell time. Even public clocks in cities used their own local time, based on the sun. Because of the sun's apparent motion, noon on one side of a large city could be at a different time on the other side of the city.

In Kansas City, Missouri, jewelers had clocks in their windows or outside their doors, each one claiming to have the correct time. Sometimes there was a twenty-five-minute difference in the times displayed, and people were confused about what time it really was. Finally the city decided to use a time ball like the ones other cities had. Everyone could see it drop, and all of Kansas City would operate by the same time.

The first time ball in the United States was established at the U.S. Naval Observatory in Washington, D.C., around 1845. Earlier in the century, time balls had been set up in British port cities to let ship captains know the exact local time. People in

Prewriting

Gather
Read an article on a topic that interests me. Jot down the 5 W's from the article.

the cities started checking the time balls for the correct time, too.

In the United States, the practice of using time balls spread quickly. Scientists began discussing the best sizes and locations. The balls were three to four feet in diameter. They were usually black, though Boston had a four-hundred-pound copper ball and Chicago's ball was red. The ball would be set up on a tall mast, usually atop a prominent building. Just before noon the ball was hoisted to the top of the mast, and then exactly at noon it was dropped to the platform below.

The time ball solved problems like the one in Kansas City, but local time still varied from city to city.

When it took days to go even a short distance of sixty miles, people didn't worry about a difference of minutes. But when the railroads started transporting people and goods more rapidly across the country, it became important to know the exact time.

Railroads had to follow rigid schedules. If a traveler's watch didn't show the correct railroad time, he just might see the train pull out of the station without him.

In 1883, the railroads started using the four standard time zones we fol-

low today (in the contiguous U.S.). The Naval Observatory was designed to provide a national time service based on these zones, and its transmission over the telegraph wires signaled the official noon in each zone to many time balls throughout the United States. Because the time balls now announced the new standard time for each zone instead of the sun time in each city, people in one part of a time zone used the same time as those in another part of that time zone.

In the 1900s, when radio made it possible to communicate long distances without the use of telegraph wires, time balls became less important in announcing the correct time. People could just turn on the radio to check the accuracy of their clocks and watches.

The last time ball that was dropped by a telegraph signal from the Naval Observatory was on top of the old Seaman's Church Institute in New York City. It ceased operation in 1967, when the building was demolished. Most other time balls had stopped operating years before that.

Today, the ball that announces the new year in Times Square is the only reminder of those bygone days.

Prewriting

Gather
Read an article on a topic that interests me. Jot down the 5 W's from the article.

your own writing

Fill in notes about the 5 W's for the article you just read. (Or you can choose another article if you want.)

5 W's

What: _____

_____

Who: _____

_____

Why: _____

_____

When: _____

_____

Where: _____

_____

RETURN Now go back to Paul's work on page 93 in the Student Edition.

Expository Writing • Summary

Prewriting

Organize   Make a main-idea table.

your own writing

Now it's time for you to practice this strategy. Circle three of the following sentences that you think are main ideas from "Dropping the Time Ball."

• Time balls can be used to count down to a new year.

• For a long time, people figured out time by looking at the sun.

• Railroad officials began using the four standard time zones to regulate train travel.

• In big cities, clocks in two sections of town might be several minutes different from each other.

• City governments introduced time balls to keep everyone on the same local time.

If you are writing about the time ball, write the sentences you circled in the chart. Then fill in two to four supporting details from the article for each one. If you have chosen another topic, fill in the chart with main ideas and details from the article you read. Continue on page 42.

Main Idea			
Detail	**Detail**	**Detail**	**Detail**

Prewriting

Organize   Make a main-idea table.

Main Idea

_____

_____

Detail	Detail	Detail	Detail
_____	_____	_____	_____
_____	_____	_____	_____
_____	_____	_____	_____
_____	_____	_____	_____
_____	_____	_____	_____

Main Idea

_____

_____

Detail	Detail	Detail	Detail
_____	_____	_____	_____
_____	_____	_____	_____
_____	_____	_____	_____
_____	_____	_____	_____
_____	_____	_____	_____

Now go back to Paul's work on page 94 in the Student Edition.

Drafting

Write Draft my summary. Keep it short, and make sure I present main ideas accurately.

Now it's time for you to practice this strategy. Here are some sentences about the information in "Dropping the Time Ball." Refer back to the article to determine the accuracy of the sentences. If a sentence is accurate, write **Accurate** on the blank. If a sentence is inaccurate, rewrite it correctly.

1. The movement of the sun was the reason it was one time on one side of a city and another time on the other side.

   _____

   _____

2. Before time balls, people rarely got confused about the time.

   _____

   _____

3. Time balls were set up in British port cities to help people in the streets keep track of time.

   _____

   _____

4. After time zones were established, a radio signaled noon to the time balls all over the country.

   _____

   _____

5. Most time balls had stopped operating long before 1967.

   _____

6. Time balls helped to keep time between one city and another.

   _____

7. The time ball in Times Square in New York is a holdover from an earlier era.

   _____

   _____

8. Railroads needed standard time zones to make their rigid schedules work.

   _____

   _____

Drafting

Write

Draft my summary. Keep it short, and make sure I present main ideas accurately.

your own writing

On the lines below, draft your own summary of "Dropping the Time Ball" or another article you've read recently.

_____

_____

_____

_____

_____

_____

_____

_____

_____

_____

_____

_____

_____

_____

_____

_____

_____

_____

_____

 Now go back to Paul's work on page 96 in the Student Edition.

ReVising

Elaborate
Check to see that I have stayed focused on my topic and not included information that is too detailed.

Now it's time for you to practice this strategy. Here is one writer's draft of a summary of the time ball article. Underline one sentence in each paragraph that either strays from the topic or is too detailed for a summary. Then on the lines below explain what is wrong with it. (The paragraphs contain some errors. You will get a chance to correct them later.)

Summary: "Dropping the Time Ball"

For a long time, people figured out time by looking at the sun. Sundials or "noon marks" were used to set watches and clocks. In big Cities, clocks in two sections of town might be several minutes diffrent from each other. For instance, on one side of Kansas City it might be 3:05 and in another neighborhood 3:09.

Time balls were interduced by city governments to keep all they're citizens on the same local time. In Boston the time ball was copper and the one in Chicago was red, but mostly time balls were black. These huge balls were put in a high place where everone could see them. When it dropped each day at noon, the correct time could be checked by people.

Railroad officeals began using four standard time zones to regulate moving trains. Eventually time zones were recognized and used all over the world. This made it easier for both they and passengers to get to stations at the right time. When radio became popular and people could check the time there, time balls gradually stopped operating.

Paragraph 1: _____

Paragraph 2: _____

Paragraph 3: _____

Remember: Use this strategy in *your own writing*

Now go back to Paul's work on page 97 in the Student Edition.

ReVising

Clarify

Make sure I have used active voice as much as possible.

Now it's time for you to practice this strategy. The sentences below, about standard time, are all in passive voice. Rewrite those that you think should be written in active voice. If a sentence cannot be changed to active voice, write **OK**. Remember that there are some times when passive voice is better to use. These times include when the doer of the action is unknown and when the doer of the action is unimportant.

1. Our nation was divided into time zones to make keeping track of travel easier.

   _____

2. Before the time zones, more than sixty different times were used by American railroads.

   _____

3. No wonder confusion was felt by people!

   _____

4. Time zones became the law of the land when the Standard Time Act of 1918 was passed by Congress.

   _____

   _____

5. Daylight Savings Time was first instituted in the United States during World War I.

   _____

Now revise this paragraph, changing passive verbs to active where possible.

   Time balls were interduced by city governments to keep all they're

   citizens on the same local time. These huge balls were put in a high place

   where everone could see them. When they dropped each day at noon,

   the correct time could be checked by people.

Remember: Use this strategy in **your own writing**

 Now go back to Paul's work on page 98 in the Student Edition.

Editing

Proofread

Check to see that pronouns are used correctly and that all antecedents are clear.

Now it's time for you to practice this strategy. Here is a summary of the article about time balls and standard time. Use the proofreading marks to correct any errors. Use a dictionary to help with spelling.

Summary: "Dropping the Time Ball"

For a long time, people figured out time by looking at the sun. Sundials or "noon marks" were used to set watches and clocks. In big Cities, clocks in two sections of town might be several minutes diffrent from each other.

City governments interduced time balls to keep all they're citizens on the same local time. These huge balls were put in a high place where everone could see them. When they dropped each day at noon, people could check the correct time.

Railroad officeals began using the four standard time zones to regulate moving trains. This made it easier for both they and passengers to get to stations at the right time. When radio became popular and people could check the time there, time balls gradually stopped operating.

Remember: Use this strategy in **your own writing**

 Now go back to Paul's work on page 100 in the Student Edition.

Using a Rubric

Use this rubric to evaluate Paul's summary on page 101 of your Student Edition. You can work with a partner.

Audience

How well does the summary convey the important points of the article to the audience?

Organization

How concisely does the writer organize and explain the article's main ideas?

Elaboration

Does the summary stay focused on main points and avoid information that is too detailed?

Clarification

Has the writer used verbs in the active voice appropriately?

your own writing

Save this rubric. Use it to check your own writing.

Conventions & Skills

How consistently does the writer provide clear antecedents and use correct pronoun forms?

Score 1 Point	Score 2 Points	Score 3 Points	Score 4 Points
(Novice)	**(Apprentice)**	**(Proficient)**	**(Distinguished)**
The writer seems to be writing mainly personal ideas instead of summarizing for an audience.	The summary includes some important points, but there are opinions mixed in that confuse the audience.	The summary includes most of the important points the audience needs to know.	The summary presents all the main points of the article, giving the audience a clear understanding of its content.
The summary presents many ideas, in a haphazard and confused way.	The summary includes a few sentences about the article, but they are not well organized.	The summary includes most of the article's main ideas, but some paragraphs are confusing.	The summary includes the article's main ideas with a paragraph about each one.
The summary is a mix of major points, details, and points not made in the article.	The summary focuses on main points but includes lots of information that is too detailed.	The summary focuses mostly on main points, but includes some information that is too detailed.	The summary focuses entirely on main points.
Extensive use of passive voice is ineffective and weakens the summary.	The writer often uses passive voice when active voice would be more appropriate.	The writer sometimes uses passive voice when active voice would be better.	The writer uses passive voice only when it is appropriate and necessary.
There are many errors with antecedents and pronoun forms.	There are several errors with antecedents and pronoun forms.	There are a few errors with antecedents and pronoun forms.	All antecedents are clear. There are no errors with pronouns.

Prewriting

Gather

Use an atlas to find a place to describe. Then research the place in three other appropriate sources.

Now it's your turn to practice this strategy with a different topic. Suppose you have decided to focus your descriptive essay in the United States. On a map of Florida, you see wavy lines covering the entire southern portion. You decide you want to answer these questions about this huge swamplike area, the Everglades:

- What is the land like?
- What kinds of plants grow there?
- What kinds of animals live there?
- What is the history of the area?

Here is a list of sources. Put a star in front of the one in each category that you think will give you the best, most useful information. Then write a brief explanation of why you chose it and how you could use it in a descriptive essay.

Internet Sites

_____ **Fourth graders in Minnesota study the Everglades**   A classroom project including students' summaries and photos of vacations in Florida and providing comparisons with Minnesota wilderness areas

_____ **Dining out in towns near the Everglades**   Sample the best of South Florida cooking in these charming restaurants.

_____ **The Ecology Channel explores the Everglades**   Accompany our tour guides as they show you the saw-grass marshes; the hummocks (small islands) covered with palms, pines, and cypresses; and other natural landforms.

Internet Site

_____

_____

Books

_____ *River of Grass,* **by Marjory Stoneman Douglas**   The classic history of the Everglades, describing the land, how it formed, its history, including Native Americans who lived there, and how it is being destroyed by development

_____ *Florida Cities,* **by Joseph Flowers**   Includes a chapter on Miami, on the edge of the Everglades

_____ *The Land and People of Southern Florida,* **by Maria Gonzalez**   Chapters by new residents of Florida, from various states and countries, on how they feel about the Everglades

Prewriting

Gather
Use an atlas to find a place to describe. Then research the place in three other appropriate sources.

Book

_____

_____

Magazine Articles

_____ **"Flying Over Florida"** Aerial photos of six regions of Florida, including the Everglades

_____ **"Animals of the Everglades"** Descriptions and photos of birds such as herons, snowbills, and snowy egrets and animals such as alligators and panthers

_____ **"Fishing Florida Waters"** A guide to the best fishing spots in Florida, with several personal accounts of fishermen's adventures

Magazine Article

_____

_____

your own writing

Use an atlas to find a place you want to write about. Jot down at least three appropriate sources here.

_____

_____

_____

_____

_____

_____

RETURN Now go back to Inez's work on page 115 in the Student Edition.

Prewriting

Organize Make a web of descriptive details.

Now it's time for you to practice this strategy. Review the Everglades sources you chose on pages 50–51, and then begin to complete the web. Fill in four main categories that your descriptive essay will cover. Then, for at least two of those categories, fill in specific descriptive details that you will include.

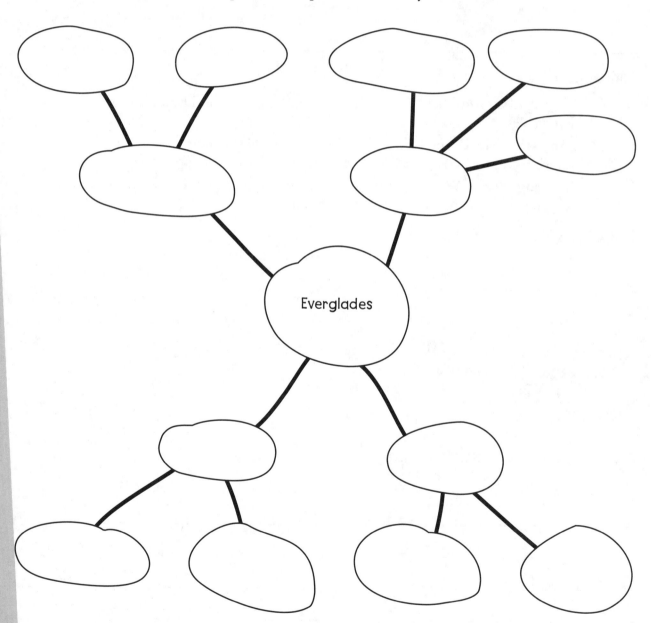

Descriptive Writing · Descriptive Essay

Prewriting

Organize Make a web of descriptive details.

your own writing

Now it's time for you to practice this strategy. Review the sources that you wrote down on page 51 for your own writing, and then begin to complete the web. Fill in four main categories that your descriptive essay will cover. Then for at least two of those categories, fill in specific descriptive details that you will include.

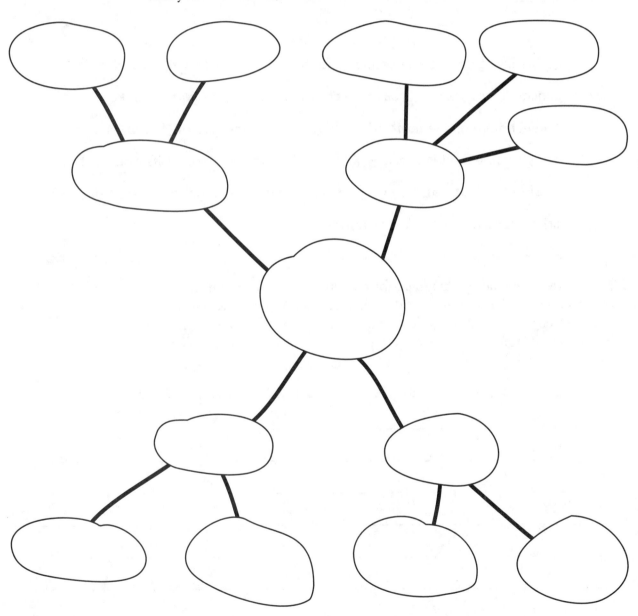

RETURN Now go back to Inez's work on page 116 in the Student Edition.

Drafting

Write
Draft my descriptive essay. Move from a general introduction to specific details and back to a general conclusion.

Now it's time for you to practice this strategy. Read the following introductory paragraph from a descriptive essay about the Everglades. (The paragraph contains some errors. You will get a chance to correct them later.)

The Everglades is one of the great naturel wonders of the world. It is a huge grassy marsh through which water flows gradual from Lake Okeechobee on the north all the way south to the gulf of Mexico. Most early people lived in harmony with its unique landscape and its abundant wildlife. The face of the everglades is changing, though, as a result of urban sprawl and other developement.

Now, write a concluding paragraph for this essay. Remember that the conclusion refers back to the introduction and often restates the information in a different way. Touch on at least some of the points that were mentioned in the introduction.

_____
_____
_____
_____
_____
_____
_____
_____

Drafting

Write
Draft my descriptive essay. Move from a general introduction to specific details and back to a general conclusion.

your own writing

Use this page to draft your own descriptive essay. Use the sources you found on page 51 and your web on page 53 to help you. Continue on another sheet of paper.

_____

_____

_____

_____

_____

_____

_____

_____

_____

_____

_____

_____

_____

_____

_____

_____

_____

_____

_____

_____

Now go back to Inez's work on page 120 in the Student Edition.

ReVising

Elaborate
Look for places to insert figurative language, including similes and metaphors.

Now it's time for you to practice the strategy. Read the following descriptions of things you might see in the Everglades. Then write a simile or metaphor that will give the reader a good mental picture of the plant or animal you're describing.

1. The great blue heron has a long neck and very long legs. The heron's neck is usually in an S-shape. The bird's body is bluish gray in color, and its head is white. About four feet tall, the heron looks like it can barely get off the ground as it begins its flight.

   _____

   _____

2. The bald cypress is a tall tree that grows in the water to more than 100 feet. It has a wide base and gets narrower as it goes up. The cypress has a silver gray color, and its short branches are often draped with air plants like hanging Spanish moss.

   _____

   _____

3. The roseate spoonbill is a bird with a pink body and a few red feathers. It has a long, flat beak that widens like a spoon at the end. This bird is about three feet long and wades in shallow waters. It builds nests in the trees using grass, branches, and leaves.

   _____

   _____

4. Saw grass is a kind of sedge, or reed, that grows in all the waters of the Everglades. Each blade has a sort of fold in the middle of it, and its edges have sharp, thin teeth. In some waters the grass grows very thickly to a height of about 10 feet. As it dies, its brown remains act as fertilizer for new grass.

   _____

   _____

   _____

Remember: Use this strategy in **your own writing**

RETURN Now go back to Inez's work on page 121 in the Student Edition.

ReVising

Clarify
Combine short, choppy sentences.
Rewrite long, confusing sentences.

Now it's time for you to practice this strategy. Read this paragraph from a descriptive essay on the Everglades.

Many birds spend at least part of the year in the Everglades. The blue heron is one of these birds. The roseate spoonbill is another of these birds. The snowy egret is still another. The blue heron is a huge bird that takes off unsteadily, like an overloaded airplane. As it digs in the waters for food, however, its tall body and graceful, S-shaped neck make a memorable picture, as does the roseate spoonbill, not quite so tall, that might also be wading and digging for food nearby. This bird's most distinctive characteristic is its long, spoon-shaped beak. Another of its distinct characteristics is its pink body with its small clump of red feathers, almost like a feather duster. Compared with the other birds the snowy egret is relatively small. It is only two feet tall. Its body is entirely white, but its feet are orange, and it uses those orange feet to disturb its prey and then it digs into the water repeatedly with its black bill until it catches what it is digging for.

ReVising

Clarify
Combine short, choppy sentences.
Rewrite long, confusing sentences.

Rewrite the paragraph on page 57. Combine and break up sentences as necessary to make the paragraph flow more smoothly and clearly.

_____

_____

_____

_____

_____

_____

_____

_____

_____

_____

_____

_____

_____

_____

_____

_____

_____

Remember:
Use this strategy in
**your own
writing**

 Now go back to Inez's work on page 122 in the Student Edition.

58

Descriptive Writing • Descriptive Essay

Editing

Proofread

Check to see that adjectives and adverbs are used correctly.

Now it's time for you to practice this strategy. Here are the first three paragraphs of a descriptive essay about the Everglades. Use the proofreading marks to correct any errors.

The Everglades is one of the great naturel wonders of the world. It is a huge grassy marsh through which water flows gradual from Lake Okeechobee on the north all the way south to the gulf of Mexico. Most early people lived in harmony with its unique landscape and its abundent wildlife. The face of the everglades is changing, though, as a result of urban sprawl and other developement.

There were people in the Everglades for thousands of years. When the spaniards arrived, in the early 1500s, they found at least three groups of Native Americans in the region. These peoples lived good on a diet of fish and used huge conch shells for tools. They lived off the land but did it little harm.

Saw grass, hummocks, and flowing water have always been the main geographical features of the Everglades. Growing to a height of about 10 feet, the saw grass has sharp edges that could cut your hands easy. It grows more thicker in some places than in others. Sometimes it is so thick that you bearly know there is water beneath it. In other places, thin patches of it stand in open waters. There you might also see hummocks, low islands covered with tropicle trees and shrubs.

Remember: Use this strategy in **your own writing**

 Now go back to Inez's work on page 124 in the Student Edition.

Using a Rubric

Use this rubric to evaluate Inez's essay on pages 125–127 of your Student Edition. You can work with a partner.

Audience

How well does the writer get and hold the audience's attention?

Organization

How clearly does the writer move from an overview of the place, through specific details, and back to a general view?

Elaboration

How effectively does the writer use figurative language to add to the description?

Clarification

How well does the writer control the length and smoothness of sentences?

your own writing

Save this rubric. Use it to check your own writing.

Conventions & Skills

How consistently does the writer use adjectives and adverbs correctly?

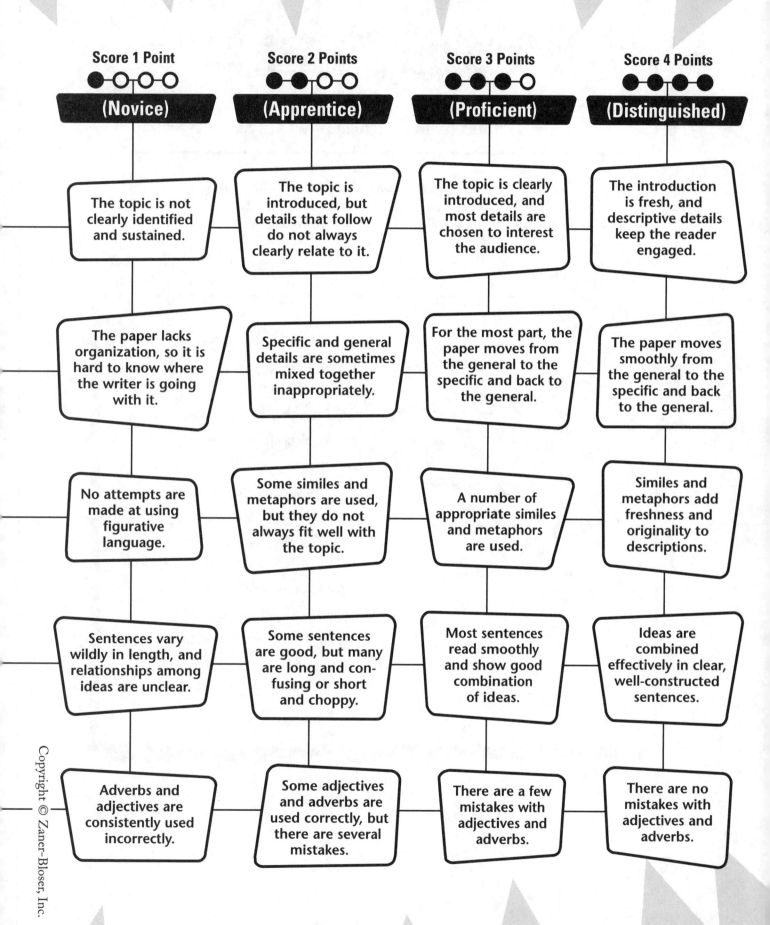

Score 1 Point
(Novice)

The topic is not clearly identified and sustained.

The paper lacks organization, so it is hard to know where the writer is going with it.

No attempts are made at using figurative language.

Sentences vary wildly in length, and relationships among ideas are unclear.

Adverbs and adjectives are consistently used incorrectly.

Score 2 Points
(Apprentice)

The topic is introduced, but details that follow do not always clearly relate to it.

Specific and general details are sometimes mixed together inappropriately.

Some similes and metaphors are used, but they do not always fit well with the topic.

Some sentences are good, but many are long and con-fusing or short and choppy.

Some adjectives and adverbs are used correctly, but there are several mistakes.

Score 3 Points
(Proficient)

The topic is clearly introduced, and most details are chosen to interest the audience.

For the most part, the paper moves from the general to the specific and back to the general.

A number of appropriate similes and metaphors are used.

Most sentences read smoothly and show good combination of ideas.

There are a few mistakes with adjectives and adverbs.

Score 4 Points
(Distinguished)

The introduction is fresh, and descriptive details keep the reader engaged.

The paper moves smoothly from the general to the specific and back to the general.

Similes and metaphors add freshness and originality to descriptions.

Ideas are combined effectively in clear, well-constructed sentences.

There are no mistakes with adjectives and adverbs.

Prewriting

Gather
Choose an aspect of nature to observe. Make notes (with sketches) of what I am observing.

One writer began taking notes after she heard a tornado warning on the radio. Her notes continued as the tornado approached, and she could see it a few miles from her home. She also made sketches of what she was seeing. Read her notes below.

- sky is sick shade of green
- fierce wind whipping through tree branches
- wind tugging at my jacket
- crows circling and cawing
- rain starts
- huge wall of clouds building in sky
- fingerlike formations poking out from clouds
- tornado forms and touches ground
- moving southwest to northeast
- sounds like jet plane
- small, dirty cloud forms at base
- signboards, trees, a mattress in the twister

PreWriting

Gather
Choose an aspect of nature to observe. Make notes (with sketches) of what I am observing.

Now it's time for you to practice this strategy with a different topic. Choose something in nature you have recently observed. On the right-hand side of the page below, write notes describing your observations. On the left-hand side of the page, draw two or three sketches of things you will include in your report.

 Now go back to Chris's work on page 137 in the Student Edition.

PReWRitiNg

Organize Make an observation chart to organize my notes.

Now it's time for you to practice this strategy. Organize the tornado notes from page 62 by listing them under the sense they appeal to. Try to include as many senses as you can. Add more details if you need to.

Topic:				
Sight	Sound	Touch	Taste	Smell

Prewriting

Organize
Make an observation chart to organize my notes.

your own writing

Now it's time for you to practice this strategy with your own topic.
Organize your notes from page 63 by listing them under the sense they appeal to. Try to include as many senses as you can. Add more details if you need to.

Topic:				
Sight	Sound	Touch	Taste	Smell

RETURN

Now go back to Chris's work on page 138 in the Student Edition.

Descriptive Writing • Observation Report

Write — Draft my report. Be sure that each body paragraph has a clear focus with strong descriptive details.

Now it's time for you to practice this strategy. Below are portions of one writer's tornado observation report. Write a topic sentence that fits with the supporting details in this paragraph. (The paragraphs contain some errors. You may correct them now or later.)

_____

_____ The sky has turned a sick shade of

green. A feirce wind is whipping around the bare branches of the trees

and trying to rip my jacket off. Several flocks of crows, as well as an

eagle, is circling and "cawing" loudly just as the rain begins.

Now write at least three descriptive details to develop the topic sentence below. Use the notes on pages 62 and 64 for ideas of what to include.

Moving from Southwest to Northeast, the twister gets noisier and more

destructive as it approaches. _____

_____

_____

_____

_____

_____

_____

_____

_____

_____

Drafting

Write

Draft my report. Be sure that each body paragraph has a clear focus with strong descriptive details.

your own writing

Now it's time for you to practice this strategy with your own topic. Draft your own observation report. Use the notes you made on pages 63 and 65. Make sure each of your paragraphs has a clear focus and descriptive details that support it. Use this page and the next.

_____

_____

_____

_____

_____

_____

_____

_____

_____

_____

_____

_____

_____

_____

_____

_____

_____

_____

_____

_____

_____

_____

Drafting

Write   Draft my report. Be sure that each body paragraph has a clear focus with strong descriptive details.

_____

_____

_____

_____

_____

_____

_____

_____

_____

_____

_____

_____

_____

_____

_____

_____

_____

_____

_____

_____

_____

 Now go back to Chris's work on page 140 in the Student Edition.

Descriptive Writing · Observation Report

Revising

Elaborate
Find appropriate pictures or create illustrations that will make my description more understandable and meaningful.

Now it's time for you to practice the strategy. Look at the photos. Choose two that you think would go with the observation report about the tornado. Under each of your choices, write a brief explanation of why you would use this photo.

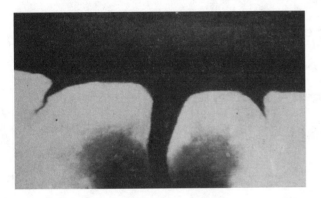

_____

_____

_____

_____

_____

_____

_____

_____

_____

_____

_____

_____

Remember: Use this strategy in **your own writing**

Now go back to Chris's work on page 141 in the Student Edition.

ReVising

Clarify Make sure that I have varied sentence length and structure.

Now it's time for you to practice the strategy. All the sentences in the paragraph below are short and have a similar structure. Combine and rewrite them to provide variety. Remember that you can add variety by beginning a sentence with an adverb, a prepositional phrase, or a dependent clause. (The paragraph contains some errors. You may correct them now or later.)

> We sees a huge wall of clouds. It is across the farm fields. It is building high and wide in the sky. Fingerlike formations begin poking out. They come through the clouds in several places. One of these finally break all the way through. It touches the ground. This is the tornado.

_____

_____

_____

_____

_____

_____

_____

_____

_____

_____

_____

_____

Remember: Use this strategy in *your own writing*

 Now go back to Chris's work on page 142 in the Student Edition.

Descriptive Writing • Observation Report

Editing

Proofread

Check to see that the subject and verb in each sentence agree.

Now it's time for you to practice this strategy. Here is part of the tornado observation report. Use the proofreading marks to correct any errors. Use a dictionary to help with spelling.

No one should be outside during a tornado, but that's where I was, driving home from school with my brother. Luckyly, we had the radio on and heard the tornado warning. We pulled under a viaduct and got out of the car. We crouched as high and as close to the side as we could. From there, this is what I observed:

The weather conditions are giving many clues that a tornado might be coming. The sky has turned a sick shade of green. A feirce wind is whipping around the bare branches of the trees and trying to rip my jacket off. Several flocks of crows, as well as an eagle, is circling and "cawing" loudly just as the rain begins.

Across the farm fields we sees a huge wall of clouds building high and wide in the sky. In several places fingerlike formations begin poking out from the clouds. Finally, one of these break all the way through and touches the ground. This is the tornado.

Moving from Southwest to Northeast, the twister gets noisier and more destructive as it approaches. A noise like that of rising jet planes fill our ears. A small, dirty cloud begins forming at the base of the tornado. As the twister comes nearer the cloud gets larger, and we can see signboards, sections of trees, and even a mattres twirling around in it.

Remember:
Use this strategy in **your own writing**

Now go back to Chris's work on page 144 in the Student Edition.

Using a Rubric

Use this rubric to evaluate Chris's observation report on page 145 of your Student Edition. You can work with a partner.

Audience

How clearly does the writer present word pictures that help the audience experience what the writer observed?

Organization

How well are main ideas organized into paragraphs with a clear focus and strong descriptive details?

Elaboration

How effectively has the writer chosen and included appropriate pictures to give more depth and meaning to verbal descriptions?

Clarification

How well has the writer kept the description lively by varying sentence length and pattern?

Conventions & Skills

How consistently has the writer used correct subject-verb agreement?

your own writing

Save this rubric. Use it to check your own writing.

Score 1 Point
(Novice)

The writer seems unaware that there is an audience for the report.

Ideas run together with no clear order or organization.

The writer includes no pictures.

Sentence patterns are the same throughout, and sentences are all about the same length.

There are many errors with subject-verb agreement.

Score 2 Points
(Apprentice)

There are few word pictures to help readers experience what the writer observed.

Some paragraphs have a clear focus, but there are few descriptive details.

The writer uses pictures, but they do not always tie clearly to the report.

The writer shows some variety in sentence length, but most sentences follow the same pattern.

There are several errors with subject-verb agreement.

Score 3 Points
(Proficient)

Clear word pictures help readers experience what the writer observed through at least one sense.

Most paragraphs have a clear focus and effective descriptive details.

The pictures clearly relate to the descriptions in the report.

The writer varies sentence pattern and length, with only a few unnatural-sounding sentences.

There are a few errors with subject-verb agreement.

Score 4 Points
(Distinguished)

Vivid word pictures help readers experience what the writer observed through several senses.

Each paragraph has a clear focus, and details create a vivid description of the experience.

Pictures clearly relate to descriptions and deepen readers' understanding.

The writer varies sentence pattern and length to create interesting, natural-sounding sentences.

There are no errors with subject-verb agreement.

Prewriting

Gather
Brainstorm to choose a problem for which I can propose a solution.

Now it's your turn to practice this strategy. Suppose you had to write a problem-solution editorial for your school newspaper. You brainstormed with your class and came up with several possible topics. Afterwards, you chose four problems that interested you and brainstormed by yourself to make some notes about them. Read through the notes.

Problem	My Ideas
○ • not enough support for the spring Clean Up/Fix Up campaign	• Nobody cleans up the graffiti on buildings or picks up trash from City Park. Can sign up volunteers here at school, give them pins to show they participated.
• Working Moms United needs more baby-sitters.	• Two of my friends' mothers are in this group, and they need help. So does Mrs. Beliza, the principal's secretary. I know a lot of kids who need to make some extra money.
○ • traffic constantly snarled at the six-corners intersection downtown	• Somebody in city government should be able to deal with this. Maybe there's an engineering department.
• not enough field trips available for kids at this school	• A lot of kids don't want field trips. There aren't too many interesting places to go around here, but maybe we could think of a few.

Prewriting

Gather
Brainstorm to choose a problem for which I can propose a solution.

Suppose you decided to choose the first topic—not enough support for the Clean Up/Fix Up campaign. Here were your reasons:

• The topic had meaning for your audience.

• You understood the problem and had some good ideas for solutions.

Analyze the topics that were not chosen. Which would have worked for the editorial, and why? Which would not have worked, and why? Write your ideas on the chart below. Use the notes from the previous page to help you evaluate.

Problem	A Good Topic?
○ • Working Moms United needs more baby-sitters.	
• traffic constantly snarled at the six-corners intersection downtown	
○ • not enough field trips available for kids at this school	

Remember: Use this strategy in **your own writing**

 Now go back to Doria's work on page 157 in the Student Edition.

Prewriting

Organize Make a problem-solution frame.

Here are some points you will want to include in your paper about the Clean Up/Fix Up campaign. Read through the list. Jot down any other points you think should be included.

- 3-4 kids sign up for certain time periods.
- a cleaner community that we can all be proud of
- City Park is filthy after the winter.
- Clean Up/Fix Up, a student organization to deal with the problem, needs help.
- Contact Clean Up/Fix Up. Find out time/volunteers the project will take.
- Everyone thinks Clean Up/Fix Up a good idea, but few people help.
- everyone's problem: a dirty community an unpleasant place to live
- Give volunteers excused school time to work.
- graffiti around our school, too
- Make "I Helped" badges for participants.
- Set up convenient tables where volunteers can sign up.
- some buildings downtown covered with graffiti
- We all use the park for sports and games.

Prewriting

Organize Make a problem-solution frame.

your own writing

Now it's time for you to practice this strategy. Organize the notes on the Clean Up/Fix Up campaign by putting each one in the Problem, Solution, or End Result part of the chart. For every point you write in the Solution section, explain a result that this solution could lead to.

Problem Box

What is the problem?

Why is it a problem?

Who has the problem?

Solution Box

Solutions

Results

End Result Box

Now go back to Doria's work on page 158 in the Student Edition.

Drafting

Write Draft my editorial. State the problem in my introduction, present the solution in the body, and sum up the results in my conclusion.

your own writing

Now it's time for you to practice this strategy. Use the space below to begin drafting your own Clean Up/Fix Up editorial. You may need to continue on a separate sheet of paper.

_____

_____

_____

_____

_____

_____

_____

_____

_____

_____

_____

_____

_____

_____

_____

_____

_____

_____

RETURN Now go back to Doria's work on page 160 in the Student Edition.

Revising

Elaborate

Check to make sure I have facts, statistics, examples, and/or anecdotes to explain the problem.

Now it's time for you to practice this strategy. Read the introductory paragraph (at the bottom of the page) from a Clean Up/Fix Up editorial. Choose the four facts from the bulleted list that will strengthen the presentation of the problem and add them to the paragraph. Rewrite or change sentences to fit the information in. (The paragraph contains some other errors. You will get a chance to correct them later.)

- There is graffiti on the sidewalks leading up to both school entrances, giving visitors a bad impression of Parkwood Middle School.
- City Park is filled with unraked leaves, old newspapers, and animal droppings.
- Some students get bored with school by springtime and cause trouble.
- Seven buildings in one block downtown have graffiti.
- There are only six active members of the Clean Up/Fix Up group, and they are all graduating this year.
- The Clean Up/Fix Up group should consider planting flowers behind the school.

Every spring, our town looks like a dezaster site. There is dirt allover.

For example, City Park, where many students play after school, is filthy.

There is also graffiti everywhere. It is on some buildings downtown and it

is around our school, too. Because a dirty comunity is an unpleasant place

to live, our school has an organization, Clean Up/Fix Up that wants to

clean up messy public areas and get rid of graffiti. Ask anyone in school,

and they will say that this organization's ideas are great. The problem is

that no one is helping out.

Remember:
Use this strategy in
your own writing

 Now go back to Doria's work on page 161 in the Student Edition.

ReVising

Clarify
Check my rationale. Get rid of any points that are unsound or do not support my solution.

Now it's time for you to practice this strategy. Here is the body paragraph from a Clean Up/Fix Up editorial. One of the numbered sentences in the paragraph is unsound and should be eliminated. Write the number of the sentence, and then write an explanation of why it should be dropped. (The paragraph contains some other errors. You will get a chance to correct them later.)

Because Clean Up/Fix Up is a school-sponsored group, the school can help to get more people involved. **1**They can start by making it clear that there will be no Sports Day for any class until 80 percent of the students volunteer. Sign-up tables should be set up in the front school entrance and near the cafeteria to make signing up easy and convienient. **2**Volunteers can sign up alone or with their friends into teams of three or four students, until the required number of students is enlisted. (Clean Up/Fix Up can tell us how many volunteers are needed, and when the work is to be done.) **3**Volunteers can sign up for the times they want to work, and as an insentive these times could be parts of work-release school days. After students have done their share of the work, they could be awarded "I Helped" badges symbols to show that they have participated in this worthy cause.

_____

_____

_____

_____

_____

Remember: Use this strategy in **your own writing**

 Now go back to Doria's work on page 162 in the Student Edition.

⌐ Indent.   ℒ Take out something.
☰ Make a capital. ⊙ Add a period.
/ Make a small letter. ⌗ New paragraph
∧ Add something.   ⓢⓟ Spelling error

Editing

Proofread
Check to see that appositives are used well and set off by commas.

Now it's time for you to practice this strategy. Here is an excerpt from a problem-solution editorial about the Clean Up/Fix Up campaign. Use the proofreading marks to correct any errors. Use a dictionary to help with spelling.

Every spring, our town looks like a dezaster site. There is dirt allover.

For example, City Park, where many students play after school, is filthy.

The park is filled with unraked leaves, old newspapers, and animal

droppings. There is also graffiti everywhere. Seven buildings on one

downtown block are covered with it, and it is around our school, too.

There is graffiti on the sidewalks leading up to both school entrances,

which certainly gives anyone visiting Parkwood Middle School a bad

impression. Because a dirty comunity is an unpleasant place to live, our

school has an organization, Clean Up/Fix Up that wants to clean up messy

public areas and get rid of graffiti. Ask anyone in school, and they will

say that this organization's ideas are great. The problem is that no one is

helping out. As of last Friday, the group had only six active members all

graduating eighth graders.

Because Clean Up/Fix Up is a school-sponsored group, the school can

help to get more people involved. Sign-up tables should be set up in the

front school entrance and near the cafeteria to make signing up easy and

convienient. Volunteers can sign up alone or with their friends into teams

of three or four students, until the required number of students is enlisted.

Remember:
Use this strategy in **your own writing**

Now go back to Doria's work on page 164 in the Student Edition.

Using a **Rubric**

Use this rubric to evaluate Doria's editorial on page 165 of your Student Edition. You can work with a partner.

Audience

How well does the writer make the audience understand the importance of the problem?

Organization

How clearly does the writer proceed from the problem to a possible solution and then to the desired end result?

Elaboration

How well has the writer built an argument supported by facts, statistics, or other strong examples?

Clarification

How consistently does the writer avoid including unsound or irrelevant facts or examples?

your own writing

Save this rubric. Use it to check your own writing.

Conventions & Skills

How well does the writer use and punctuate appositives (phrases describing nouns)?

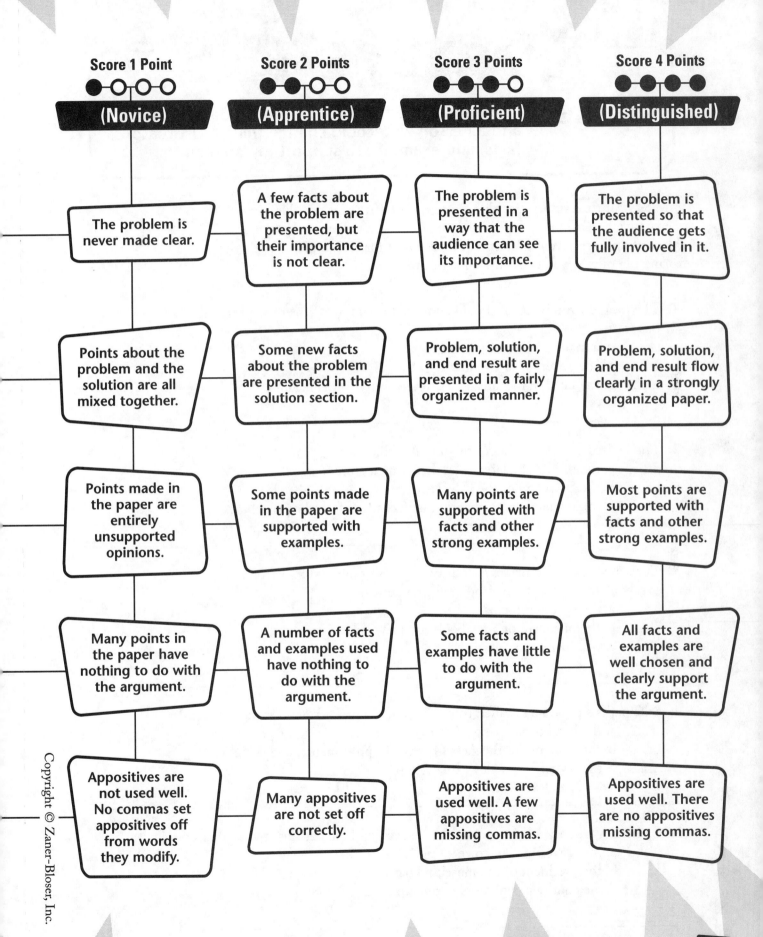

Score 1 Point
● ○ ○ ○
(Novice)

Score 2 Points
● ● ○ ○
(Apprentice)

Score 3 Points
● ● ● ○
(Proficient)

Score 4 Points
● ● ● ●
(Distinguished)

The problem is never made clear.

A few facts about the problem are presented, but their importance is not clear.

The problem is presented in a way that the audience can see its importance.

The problem is presented so that the audience gets fully involved in it.

Points about the problem and the solution are all mixed together.

Some new facts about the problem are presented in the solution section.

Problem, solution, and end result are presented in a fairly organized manner.

Problem, solution, and end result flow clearly in a strongly organized paper.

Points made in the paper are entirely unsupported opinions.

Some points made in the paper are supported with examples.

Many points are supported with facts and other strong examples.

Most points are supported with facts and other strong examples.

Many points in the paper have nothing to do with the argument.

A number of facts and examples used have nothing to do with the argument.

Some facts and examples have little to do with the argument.

All facts and examples are well chosen and clearly support the argument.

Appositives are not used well. No commas set appositives off from words they modify.

Many appositives are not set off correctly.

Appositives are used well. A few appositives are missing commas.

Appositives are used well. There are no appositives missing commas.

Prewriting

Gather

Choose an issue that I have a strong opinion about, and a person who could change things. List reasons, facts, and examples to support my opinion.

Now it's your turn to practice this strategy. Look at these possible topics for a persuasive letter. Then put a check before the best audience—person or organization to receive the letter—of those listed for each topic. Write a short explanation of why you chose the audience you did.

1. The local downtown mall should be turned back into a street with car and bus traffic.
   _____ a. a manufacturer of passenger buses
   _____ b. the governor of the state
   _____ c. the head of the Business Owners' Improvement Fund

   _____

2. The United States should get rid of dollar bills.
   _____ a. the owner of a large local department store
   _____ b. the Secretary of the U.S. Treasury
   _____ c. the manager of a cafeteria that has a lot of vending machines

   _____

3. The school should provide us with two copies of our textbooks, one to use at school and one to keep at home for homework.
   _____ a. the school principal
   _____ b. the president of a textbook company
   _____ c. your parent or guardian

   _____

4. Bike paths should be installed throughout Tremens Park and Prairie.
   _____ a. the head of the park district
   _____ b. the head of the Business Owners' Improvement Fund
   _____ c. the owner of Owsley's Bike Shop

   _____

5. Catherton County Museum should have evening hours at least two nights a week.
   _____ a. the mayor of your town
   _____ b. the president of the museum board
   _____ c. the county parent-teacher organization

   _____

Prewriting

Gather

Choose an issue that I have a strong opinion about, and a person who could change things. List reasons, facts, and examples to support my opinion.

your own writing

Now it's time for you to practice this strategy with your own topic. Think of a topic or issue about which you have a strong opinion. Use a topic from page 84 if you want. Make notes about the issue. Decide who should receive your letter. Try to organize your notes into reasons, facts, and examples.

Who will get the letter: _____

Reasons: _____

_____

_____

_____

_____

_____

Facts: _____

_____

_____

_____

_____

Examples: _____

_____

_____

_____

_____

RETURN Now go back to Leon's work on page 175 in the Student Edition.

Prewriting

Organize
Make a persuasion map to organize reasons, facts, and examples to support my call to action.

Now it's your turn to practice this strategy. One writer decided to write a persuasive letter to the Secretary of the Treasury about why dollar bills should be replaced. Here are some of that writer's reasons, as well as some facts and examples to support those reasons. Use the information below to complete the persuasion map on the next page. Follow these steps:

1. Insert the reasons in the order you think they should be dealt with in the letter.
2. Insert the facts and examples with the reasons that they support. If you can, add one fact or example of your own to support each reason.
3. Briefly summarize your call to action—what you want the receiver of the letter to do.

Reasons

- With no dollar bills, people will use dollar coins.
- Other countries don't have small bills, just coins.
- New dollar bills have to be frequently reprinted.

Facts/Examples

- Canada and other countries: small bills taken out of circulation
- costs a lot to keep reprinting dollars
- dollar bills used a lot—wear out
- coins convenient for vending machines, parking meters
- no alternatives; people have gotten used to coins
- dollar coins: lightweight and easy to identify

Copyright © Zaner-Bloser, Inc.

Prewriting

Organize

Make a persuasion map to organize reasons, facts, and examples to support my call to action.

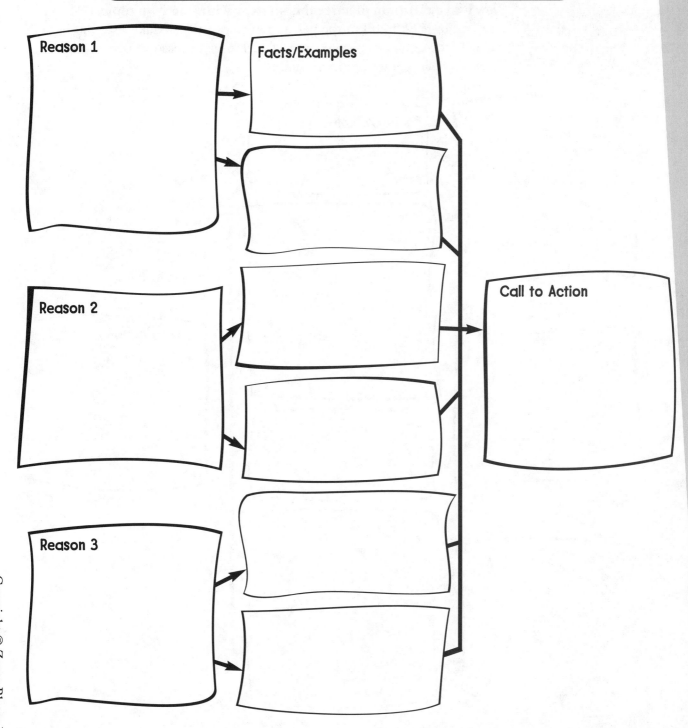

Reason 1

Facts/Examples

Reason 2

Call to Action

Reason 3

Prewriting

Organize

Make a persuasion map to organize reasons, facts, and examples to support my call to action.

your own writing

Now it's your turn to practice this strategy with your own topic. Use your notes on page 85 to fill in the persuasion chart below. Make sure you have enough facts and examples to support each of your reasons. Use another sheet of paper if you need more space.

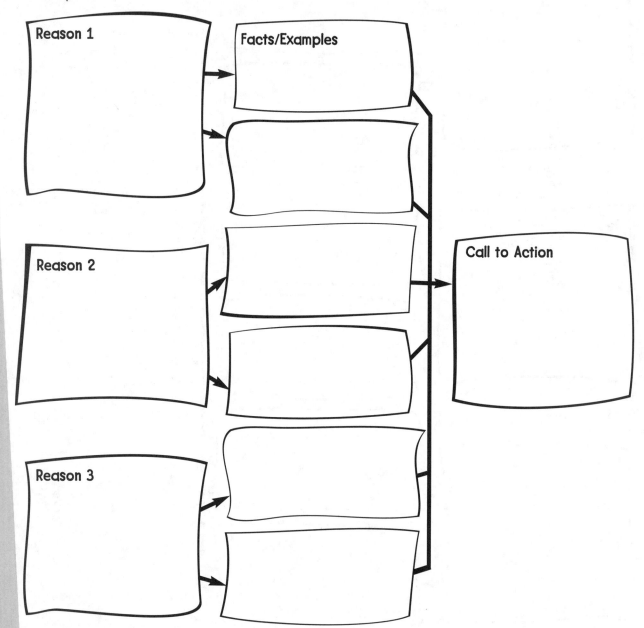

Reason 1

Facts/Examples

Reason 2

Reason 3

Call to Action

RETURN Now go back to Leon's work on page 176 in the Student Edition.

Persuasive Writing • Persuasive Letter

Drafting

Write   Draft the body of my letter. Use topic sentences to present the reasons for my opinion.

your own writing

Now it's time for you to practice this strategy. Use this page and the next to plan and draft the body of a persuasive letter. Write a brief opening paragraph stating your opinion and the background or experience that led you to it. Then, using your persuasion map on page 88, write topic sentences for your reason paragraphs and a brief call-to-action paragraph.

Opinion Paragraph:

_____

_____

_____

_____

_____

_____

_____

Topic Sentence/Reason 1:

_____

_____

_____

_____

Drafting

Write Draft the body of my letter. Use topic sentences to present the reasons for my opinion.

Topic Sentence/Reason 2:

_____

_____

_____

_____

Topic Sentence/Reason 3:

_____

_____

_____

_____

_____

Call-to-Action Paragraph

_____

_____

_____

_____

_____

_____

 Now go back to Leon's work on page 178 in the Student Edition.

Persuasive Writing • Persuasive Letter

Revising

Elaborate

Make sure detail sentences in my paragraphs provide strong support for the topic sentence.

Now it's time for you to practice this strategy. Here is a topic sentence for one writer's persuasive letter about replacing dollar bills, followed by a list of possible details. Circle the three details that support the topic sentence. Use them to write sentences that develop a paragraph.

Topic Sentence:

I believe that with no dollar bills around, people would see the advantages of our Sacagawea dollar coins and begin to use them.

- already can be used in some vending machines and parking meters

- coins lightweight and easy to carry around

- contest held to design the best image for these coins

- gold color makes them easy to find in a handful of change

- be proud of coins that show part of our heritage

I believe that with no dollar bills around, people would see the

advantages of our Sacagawea dollar coins and begin to use them.

_____

_____

_____

_____

_____

_____

_____

_____

Remember: Use this strategy in **your own writing**

Now go back to Leon's work on page 179 in the Student Edition.

ReVising

Clarify
Check to make sure that I have not misused homophones or other easily confused words.

Now it's time for you to practice this strategy. There are several errors with homophones and other easily confused words in the following paragraphs. Revise the paragraphs, correcting these errors. (The paragraphs contain some other errors as well. You may correct them now or later.)

I work part-time as a cashier in a grocery store for my parents, and I freequently need to give people seven or ate dollar bills in change. These bills seem like a big nuisence to me, and I think that you should take them out of circulation. You could do this without no inconvenience to people. Here are my reasons for thinking as I due.

To begin with, most of the dollar bills I sea aren't barely usable and need to be replaced. I no from my experience as a cashier that dollar bills are used all the time, and that is the reason they look so worn out. it must cost a lot of money to constently reprint these bills. Their must be a better way then that.

I recently red that many countries use coins, not paper money, for small denominations. I no that Canada and England have done this, and it has saved them a large amount in printing costs.

Remember: Use this strategy in *your own writing*

 Now go back to Leon's work on page 180 in the Student Edition.

Persuasive Writing • Persuasive Letter

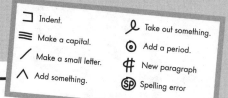

Proofread — Make sure business-letter form is correct and that there are no double negatives.

Now it's time for you to practice this strategy. Here is part of one writer's persuasive letter. Use the proofreading marks to correct any errors. Use a dictionary to help with spelling.

735 W. Perkins Boulevard

Pierre, SD 57501

August, 22, 20--

The Honorable Paul O'Neill

Secretary of the treasury

United States Treasury

1500 Pennsylvania Avenue NW

Washington, DC, 20220

dear Secretary O'Neill:

   I work part-time as a cashier in a grocery store for my parents, and I freequently need to give people seven or eight dollar bills in change. These bills seem like a big nuisence to me, and I think that you should take them out of circulation. You could do this without no inconvenience to people. Here are my reasons for thinking as I do.

   To begin with, most of the dollar bills I see aren't barely usable and need to be replaced. I know from my experience as a cashier that dollar bills are used all the time, and that is the reason they look so worn out. it must cost a lot of money to constently reprint these bills. There must be a better way than that.

Now go back to Leon's work on page 182 in the Student Edition.

Remember: Use this strategy in **your own writing**

Using a Rubric

Use this rubric to evaluate Leon's letter on pages 183–185 of your Student Edition. You can work with a partner.

Audience

How quickly and clearly is the writer's opinion presented to the reader?

Organization

How consistently does the writer use paragraphs with strong, clear topic sentences to present reasons for the opinion?

Elaboration

How effectively do detail sentences support topic sentences in paragraphs?

Clarification

How clear and correct is the writer's use of homophones and other confusing words?

Conventions & Skills

How carefully does the writer follow correct business-letter form? How well does the writer avoid double negatives?

your own writing

Save this rubric. Use it to check your own writing.

Score 1 Point	Score 2 Points	Score 3 Points	Score 4 Points
●━○━○	●━●━○━○	●━●━●━○	●━●━●━●
(Novice)	**(Apprentice)**	**(Proficient)**	**(Distinguished)**

The writer's opinion is never made clear to the reader.	The writer's opinion is not made clear to the reader until the end of the letter.	The writer's opinion is given in a somewhat long introductory paragraph.	The writer's opinion is given in a brief, clear introductory paragraph.
Paragraphs generally do not have topic sentences.	Paragraphs have topic sentences, but they don't always give reasons for the writer's opinion.	Paragraphs have topic sentences, and most give reasons for the writer's opinion.	Paragraphs consistently have topic sentences that give reasons for the writer's opinion.
Details are mostly unrelated to topic sentences.	Details sometimes support topic sentences.	Most details support topic sentences, but a few are unrelated.	All details provide strong support for topic sentences.
The writer uses the wrong word many times.	The writer has several errors with homophones and other confusing words.	The writer occasionally uses the wrong word.	The writer always uses the correct homophone or other easily confused word.
The letter is missing several parts, and there are many double negatives.	The letter is missing at least one part, and there are several double negatives.	The letter has all basic parts, but there are a few errors in them and with double negatives.	The letter has all basic parts, and there are no errors with them or with double negatives.

Prewriting

Gather
Choose a condition in nature that causes certain effects. Do research and take notes about it.

Now it's your turn to practice this strategy with a different topic. Read the following article. Then follow the directions on the next page.

The Old World climbing fern is a plant that came originally from Asia and Australia. Now it is found in the United States. It has gotten into the Everglades, the most important natural waterway in Florida, and covers more than 10 percent of the area. It is an invasive plant, one that grows and grows until it covers everything in its path.

The fast-growing plant has thick, strong vines. These vines form a mat so dense that it can actually alter the flow of stream waters. The potential damage it could do to the Everglades is alarming.

The climbing fern looks beautiful. However, it drapes itself over trees, bushes, and other plants and smothers them. They cannot get any sunlight, and they die. When the fern's leaves die off, they turn dry and brown. If they catch fire, they also burn the plants and ground that they cover.

Insects, birds, and other animals are part of any natural environment. If the plants that they are used to feeding on are no longer there—because the climbing fern has displaced them—then many of these animal species move, too.

People are looking for ways to get rid of the climbing fern. In the meantime, Floridians are asked to notify authorities about places where they see it beginning to grow.

Prewriting

Gather

Choose a condition in nature that causes certain effects. Do research and take notes about it.

your own writing

Write notes about the article you just read on page 96 of this book or about another topic of your choice. As you work, be sure that you have noted one cause and at least three effects.

RETURN Now go back to Chantrelle's work on page 197 in the Student Edition.

Prewriting

Organize

Make a cause-and-effect chain to organize my notes.

your own writing

Now it's time for you to practice this strategy. Use your notes on page 97 to decide on three effects you want to cover in your paper. Fill in the cause-and-effect chain, putting the effects in the order you will discuss them.

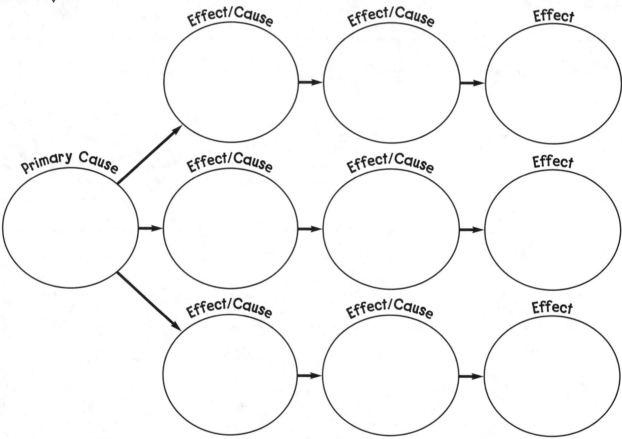

Now go back to Chantrelle's work on page 198 in the Student Edition.

Write Draft my report. Start by composing my thesis statement.

your own writing

Now it's time for you to practice this strategy. Use your cause-and-effect chain and, if you're writing about the climbing fern, information from the article on page 96. Write an opening paragraph for your cause-and-effect report. End the paragraph with a thesis statement. Follow these guidelines:

- Lead up to the thesis statement with interesting facts or information.
- In the thesis statement, clearly identify the cause on which the report will focus.

You will work on topic sentences on the next page.

_____

_____

_____

_____

_____

_____

_____

_____

_____

_____

_____

_____

_____

_____

_____

Drafting

Write — Draft my report. Start by composing my thesis statement.

On the lines below, write three topic sentences for your effect paragraphs. Remember to identify the effect clearly in each topic sentence.

Effect/Topic Sentence 1:

_____

_____

_____

_____

_____

Effect/Topic Sentence 2:

_____

_____

_____

_____

_____

Effect/Topic Sentence 3:

_____

_____

_____

_____

_____

 Now go back to Chantrelle's work on page 200 in the Student Edition.

Expository Writing • Cause-and-Effect Report

ReVising

Elaborate
Make sure I have included enough supporting details to show how a cause leads to certain effects.

Now it's time for you to practice this strategy. Here is the beginning of one writer's effect paragraph from a cause-and-effect report about the climbing fern. Following it are five possible supporting details. Choose two details below the paragraph that relate most closely to the information in the paragraph. Add them in an order that makes sense to you. The paragraph and details have some errors. You will have a chance to fix them later.

The most common complaint about the climbing fern is that it kills off other plants. The fern has a main stemlike leef that can grow as much as 100 feet long. Anywhere along this leaf other leafy branches can devolop. The climbing fern grows fast and is soon draped over and around plants, bushes, and even trees. _____

_____

_____

_____

_____

- Because its so long and heavy, it can cause even trees to collapse.
- Because it has spores that can be carried on the wind, you cannot tell where it will grow next.
- When it was first imported from Asia and Australia, people used it as an ornamental plant.
- Because frost kills it off, it will not grow north of Central Florida.
- Because its so thick and leafy, it creates a dense shade that kills anything growing underneath it.

Remember:
Use this strategy in *your own writing*

RETURN Now go back to Chantrelle's work on page 201 in the Student Edition.

ReVising

Clarify

Check to see that I have used transition words to make cause-and-effect relationships clear.

Now it's time for you to practice this strategy. Here is another paragraph from the report about the climbing fern. Rewrite the paragraph, adding at least three transition words or phrases to make relationships clear. (The paragraph contains some errors. You can correct them now or later.)

Remember that a transition word or phrase ties ideas together. Common transition words include *because, effect, so, since, therefore, as a result, after, while, then, first, second, third, next, before, once,* and *also.*

> The climbing fern dosen't affect just plants. It affects animals. It substitutes itself for local plants. The insects and other animals that feed on these plants cant eat. They leave the area or die. Loxahatchee is a wildlife area with tree islands. These islands used to be songbirds special refuge. Now the climbing fern has covered the islands. Very few songbirds gather there now.

_____

_____

_____

_____

_____

_____

_____

_____

_____

_____

_____

Remember:
Use this strategy in
your own writing

 Now go back to Chantrelle's work on page 202 in the Student Edition.

Expository Writing • Cause-and-Effect Report

⌐ Indent.	ℓ Take out something.
☰ Make a capital.	⊙ Add a period.
/ Make a small letter.	# New paragraph
∧ Add something.	SP Spelling error

Editing

Proofread   Make sure I've used apostrophes correctly in possessive nouns and contractions.

Now it's time for you to practice this strategy. Here is part of one writer's cause-and-effect report on the Old World climbing fern. Use the proofreading marks to correct any errors. Use a dictionary to help with spelling.

Beautiful but Deadly

Chances are that you've heard about kudzu or zebra mussels. Both are species that get into an area they are not native to and then take it over. One invasive species that you may not know of has now shown up in central and southern Florida. Its the Old World climbing fern, and its causing pretty severe problems wherever it grows.

The most common complaint about the climbing fern is that it kills off other plants. The fern has a main stemlike leef that can grow as much as 100 feet long. Anywhere along this leaf other leafy branches can devolop. The climbing fern grows fast and is soon draped over and around plants, bushes, and even trees. Because its so thick and leafy, it creates a dense shade that kills anything growing underneath it. Because its so long and heavy, it can cause even trees to collapse.

The climbing fern dosen't just affect plants. It also affects animals. Because it substitutes itself for local plants, the insecs and other animals that feed on these plants cant eat, so they leave the area or die. Loxahatchee is a wildlife area with tree islands. These islands used to be songbirds special refuge. Now the climbing fern has covered the islands. As a result, very few songbirds gather there now.

Remember:
Use this strategy in
your own writing

Now go back to Chantrelle's work on page 204 in the Student Edition.

Using a Rubric

Use this rubric to evaluate Chantrelle's report on page 205 of your Student Edition. You can work with a partner.

Audience

How clearly does the writer's thesis statement let the reader know the topic on which the paper will focus?

Organization

How adequately does the writer select and organize effects that result from specific causes?

Elaboration

How effectively does the writer use supporting details to show how a cause leads to a certain effect?

Clarification

How appropriately does the writer use transition words to emphasize cause-and-effect relationships?

your own writing

Save this rubric. Use it to check your own writing.

Conventions & Skills

How carefully and correctly does the writer use apostrophes?

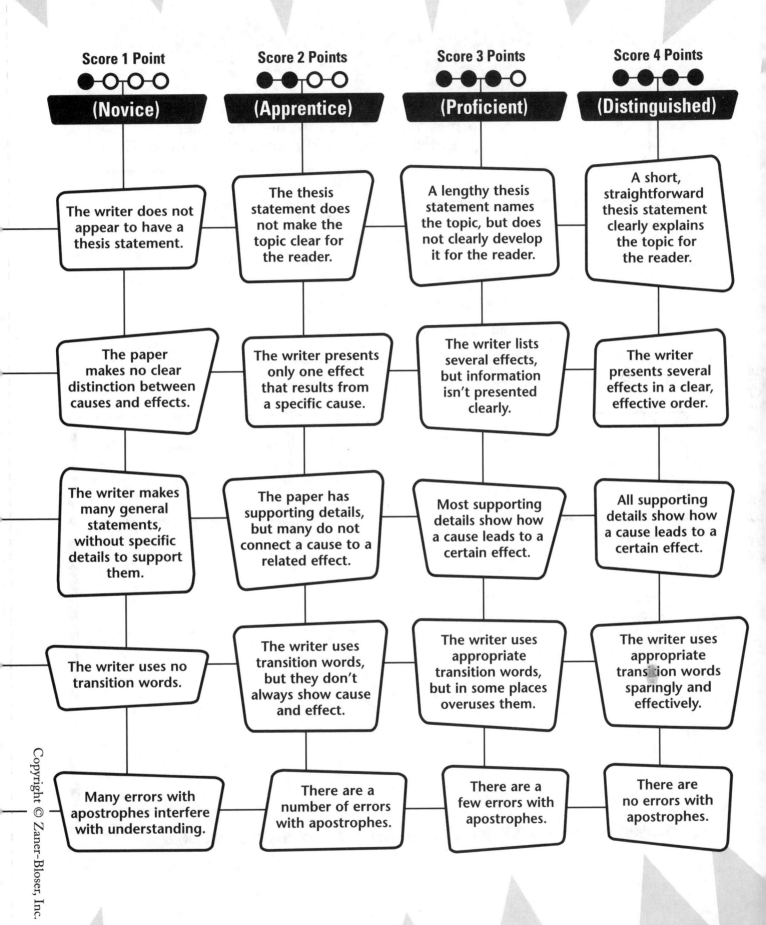

Score 1 Point

(Novice)

The writer does not appear to have a thesis statement.

The paper makes no clear distinction between causes and effects.

The writer makes many general statements, without specific details to support them.

The writer uses no transition words.

Many errors with apostrophes interfere with understanding.

Score 2 Points

(Apprentice)

The thesis statement does not make the topic clear for the reader.

The writer presents only one effect that results from a specific cause.

The paper has supporting details, but many do not connect a cause to a related effect.

The writer uses transition words, but they don't always show cause and effect.

There are a number of errors with apostrophes.

Score 3 Points

(Proficient)

A lengthy thesis statement names the topic, but does not clearly develop it for the reader.

The writer lists several effects, but information isn't presented clearly.

Most supporting details show how a cause leads to a certain effect.

The writer uses appropriate transition words, but in some places overuses them.

There are a few errors with apostrophes.

Score 4 Points

(Distinguished)

A short, straightforward thesis statement clearly explains the topic for the reader.

The writer presents several effects in a clear, effective order.

All supporting details show how a cause leads to a certain effect.

The writer uses appropriate transition words sparingly and effectively.

There are no errors with apostrophes.

Prewriting

Gather

Choose a topic and make a K-W-S chart. Get information from the Internet and other appropriate sources and record it on note cards.

Now it's your turn to practice this strategy with another topic. Suppose you want to learn more about synesthesia (sin' · is · **thee** · zhuh). This is a condition where a person experiences things through two senses at once. For example, a musical note (a sound) may taste like broccoli. Use the list of sources below and your own curiosity to fill in the K-W-S chart.

- article by Susan Hornick that includes a history of synesthesia
- book by Albert Toomy about what it's like to have synesthesia
- article by Tom Lewis about famous people with synesthesia
- Web site article that explains synesthesia in easy-to-understand terms

What I Know	What I Want to Know	Sources to Answer My Questions
Other senses besides taste and sound may be combined.		
People have known about it for a long time but didn't know what to make of it.		
Certain kinds of people are more likely to have it.		

Prewriting

Gather
Choose a topic and make a K-W-S chart. Get information from the Internet and other appropriate sources and record it on note cards.

Continue practicing the strategy. Here is part of an article on synesthesia. After you read it, write a note card about it. Include the following:

- a label identifying the topic

- information relating to the topic (either summarized or directly quoted)

- the source of the information

"In 1812, Dr. G.T.L. Sachs published the first scientific treatise on synesthesia. In it, he described how he and his sister experienced vivid color sensations when seeing, hearing or even thinking about various vowels, consonants, names and numbers. For the next 70 years, the only synesthetes to describe their symptoms publicly were doctors and researchers whose curiosity about their conditions outweighed their fear of being ridiculed or labeled insane."

—Susan Hornik, "For Some, Pain Is Orange"
Smithsonian, February 2001, page 48

Prewriting

Gather

Choose a topic and make a K-W-S chart. Get information from the Internet and other appropriate sources and record it on note cards.

your own writing

Now it's your turn to practice this strategy with your own topic. Choose a topic that interests you and begin gathering information about it. You may want to write about something in social studies or science. Fill in the K-W-S chart below.

What I Know	What I Want to Know	Sources to Answer My Questions

Expository Writing • Research Report

Prewriting

Gather
Choose a topic and make a K-W-S chart. Get information from the Internet and other appropriate sources and record it on note cards.

your own writing

Write at least one note card about the topic you chose on page 108. Include the following:

- a label identifying your topic
- information relating to the topic (either summarized or directly quoted)
- the source of the information

_____

_____

_____

_____

_____

_____

_____

_____

_____

_____

_____

_____

_____

_____

RETURN Now go back to Travis's work on page 218 in the Student Edition.

Prewriting

Organize

Make an outline to organize the information on my note cards. Distinguish between fact and opinion as I organize.

Now it's your turn to practice this strategy. After reviewing her note cards, one writer decided to include the points below in an outline for a report on synesthesia. Use them to complete the outline of the body of the report on the next page. Begin by filling in main ideas next to Roman numerals. Then add paragraph topics and supporting details. You may also find it helpful to refer back to the K-W-S chart on page 106 as you work.

Main Ideas

- History of research into synesthesia
- Famous people who have it
- How it works

Paragraph Topics

- Present-day researchers looking for causes in the brain
- Affects different kinds of people in different ways
- David Hockney, painter
- Earliest research about 200 years ago

Supporting Details

- famous novelist who saw letters as colors
- early idea: people with it were crazy
- one opinion: input from many senses blends in one region of brain
- affects people all over the world
- paints colors of music he is listening to
- letters associated with specific colors
- used music to get right colors for opera sets
- synesthesia sign of artistic temperament

Prewriting

Organize

Make an outline to organize the information on my note cards. Distinguish between fact and opinion as I organize.

I. _____
   A. Various senses may be combined
      1. violin sound may feel like a soft touch on the face
      2. _____
      3. sound may bring up a taste
   B. _____
      1. affects women more often than men
      2. _____
      3. two people won't necessarily see the same letter with the same color

II. _____
   A. _____
      1. first paper published in 1812 (Dr. Sachs)
      2. _____
      3. many people afraid to admit they had it
   B. Around 1900, became almost a fad
      1. many artists claimed they had synesthesia
      2. _____

III. _____
   A. Vladimir Nabokov, writer
      1. _____
      2. letter i had pistachio-green color
      3. mother saw same letters as different colors
   B. _____
      1. _____
      2. used music to get right colors for opera sets

Prewriting

Organize

Make an outline to organize the information on my note cards. Distinguish between fact and opinion as I organize.

your own writing

Now it's time for you to practice this strategy with your own topic.
Review the information in your K-W-S chart on page 108 and your note card on page 109. Use that information to write an outline for a research report on your topic. You will probably have to do more research before you begin.

_____

_____

_____

_____

_____

_____

_____

_____

_____

_____

_____

_____

_____

_____

_____

_____

_____

_____

Prewriting

Organize

Make an outline to organize the information on my note cards. Distinguish between fact and opinion as I organize.

_____

_____

_____

_____

_____

_____

_____

_____

_____

_____

_____

_____

_____

_____

_____

_____

_____

_____

_____

 Now go back to Travis's work on page 220 in the Student Edition.

Drafting

Write Draft my research report. Be sure to include a strong introduction, body, and conclusion.

Now it's your turn to practice this strategy. Write a good opening paragraph for a report on synesthesia. You might include some of these facts to make your introduction more interesting.

- to some with synesthesia, the smell of mint feels like glass
- most common combination: numbers or letters have distinct colors
- sometimes referred to as "colored learning"
- synesthesia = syn, Greek for "together," + aisthesis, Greek for "perception"
- Al Toomy knew he had synesthesia since he was seven.

_____

_____

_____

_____

_____

_____

_____

_____

_____

_____

_____

_____

_____

_____

_____

Expository Writing • Research Report

Drafting

Write Draft my research report. Be sure to include a strong introduction, body, and conclusion.

your own writing

Now it's time to practice this strategy with your own topic. Have your outline on pages 112–113 approved by your teacher. Make changes if necessary. Then, following your outline, use this page and the next to begin drafting your report.

_____

_____

_____

_____

_____

_____

_____

_____

_____

_____

_____

_____

_____

_____

_____

_____

_____

_____

DRafting

Write   Draft my research report. Be sure to include a strong introduction, body, and conclusion.

RETURN   Now go back to Travis's work on page 224 in the Student Edition.

Expository Writing • Research Report

Revising

Elaborate
Add quotes and information from experts to help make important points.

Now it's time for you to practice this strategy. Here is a paragraph from a research report about synesthesia and three possible sources for the information in it. Choose the two sources that seem to relate to the paragraph, and add identification about them to the paragraph.

Possible sources:

- Susan Hornick, writing about the unity between nature and man
- Tom Lewis, writing about famous people with synesthesia
- Unmesh Kher, writing about the appeal of synesthesia to artists

Late in the nineteenth century, the public's reaction to synesthesia began to change. Some people began to think that synesthesia was wonderful. It had great appeal for the artists of the period. Artists were attracted to the merging of the senses. This idea "fit perfectly with the Romantic view of the unity of man and nature." And so, for a time, synesthesia became quite popular. Some people would even pretend they had it, even if they didn't. As a matter of fact, people claiming to have synesthesia seemed to be everywhere.

Remember: Use this strategy in **your own writing**

Now go back to Travis's work on page 226 in the Student Edition.

ReVising

Clarify
Make sure that I have summarized accurately and not plagiarized information.

Now it's time for you to practice this strategy. Read this source material about synesthesia from Tom Lewis's book. Then read the two excerpts from a research report. Tell what is wrong with each one and how you would fix it.

> When my brother Tad was nine years old, he began to realize that he saw the world differently than his friends and the rest of the family did. One day, walking home from school, he was talking to a classmate about some math concepts they were studying. When he asked his friend "Don't you think 9's are a nice shade of blue?" the friend looked at him like he was crazy. Later, he told our mother how strangely his friend had reacted. She said, "Well, my 9's don't have any special color either!" Tad learned a lesson or two that day.

Excerpt 1. Tad Lewis found out about his synesthesia when he was nine years old. When he asked his friend "Don't you think 9's are a nice shade of blue?" his friend looked at him like he was crazy. Later, his mother told him, "Well, my 9's don't have any special color either!"

_____

_____

_____

Excerpt 2. Tom Lewis found out about his brother Tad's synesthesia when they were both nine years old. Tad told his mother and his brother about how certain letters had colors, but neither of them had the same experience. Later, he told a friend, but the friend didn't really understand him either.

_____

_____

_____

Remember: Use this strategy in **your own writing**

 Now go back to Travis's work on page 228 in the Student Edition.

Expository Writing • Research Report

Editing

Proofread

Check capitalization and punctuation of proper nouns, proper adjectives, abbreviations, and initials.

Now it's time for you to practice this strategy. Here is the bibliography from a report on synesthesia. Rewrite it, correcting errors with proper nouns, proper adjectives, abbreviations, and initials. Remember to put sources in alphabetical order.

Hornick, Susan. "For some, Pain Is Orange." <u>Smithsonian</u> February 2001: 48.

Toomy, Albert J., jr. <u>I Hear Colors</u>. Springfield: stardust Press, 1999.

Lewis, Tom. "Famous People with Synesthesia." Synesthesia. 10 July 2001.

  <http://www.synesthesia.org>

"Ask Dr Sparks: Ten Minutes To Understanding Synesthesia." <u>Timmons</u>

  <u>Weekly Magazine</u> 10 April 2002: 18.

_____

_____

_____

_____

_____

_____

_____

_____

_____

_____

_____

Remember: Use this strategy in **your own writing**

 Now go back to Travis's work on page 230 in the Student Edition.

Using a Rubric

Use this rubric to evaluate Travis's research report on pages 231–233 in the Student Edition. You can work with a partner.

Audience

How successfully does the writer show awareness of the audience in presenting facts and ideas?

Organization

How effectively does the writer introduce, develop, and then summarize the topic of the report?

Elaboration

How accurately and appropriately has the writer quoted authorities and identified sources of information?

Clarification

How well has the writer summarized sources' ideas and presented them in his or her own words?

Conventions & Skills

How accurately are proper nouns, proper adjectives, and abbreviations capitalized and punctuated?

your own writing

Save this rubric. Use it to check your own writing.

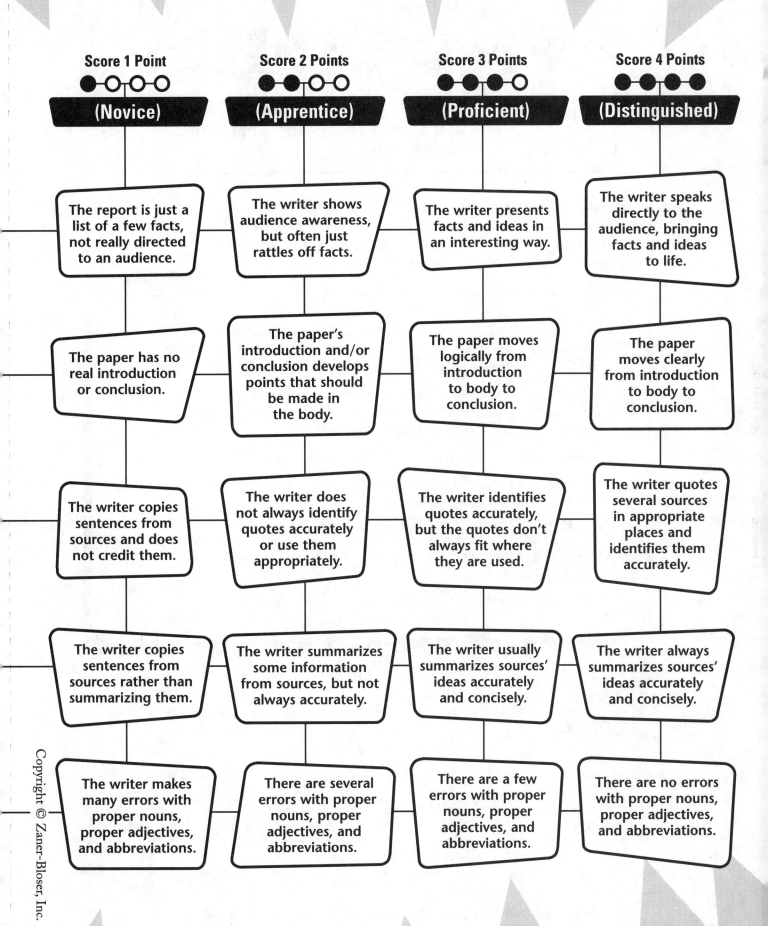

Score 1 Point (Novice)

The report is just a list of a few facts, not really directed to an audience.

The paper has no real introduction or conclusion.

The writer copies sentences from sources and does not credit them.

The writer copies sentences from sources rather than summarizing them.

The writer makes many errors with proper nouns, proper adjectives, and abbreviations.

Score 2 Points (Apprentice)

The writer shows audience awareness, but often just rattles off facts.

The paper's introduction and/or conclusion develops points that should be made in the body.

The writer does not always identify quotes accurately or use them appropriately.

The writer summarizes some information from sources, but not always accurately.

There are several errors with proper nouns, proper adjectives, and abbreviations.

Score 3 Points (Proficient)

The writer presents facts and ideas in an interesting way.

The paper moves logically from introduction to body to conclusion.

The writer identifies quotes accurately, but the quotes don't always fit where they are used.

The writer usually summarizes sources' ideas accurately and concisely.

There are a few errors with proper nouns, proper adjectives, and abbreviations.

Score 4 Points (Distinguished)

The writer speaks directly to the audience, bringing facts and ideas to life.

The paper moves clearly from introduction to body to conclusion.

The writer quotes several sources in appropriate places and identifies them accurately.

The writer always summarizes sources' ideas accurately and concisely.

There are no errors with proper nouns, proper adjectives, and abbreviations.

Prewriting

Gather
Read and analyze the writing prompt. Make sure I understand what I am supposed to do.

Now it's time to practice this strategy with a different topic. Carefully read the prompt below. Think about what it asks you to do. Circle the part of the prompt that describes the task. Then circle the key words that tell you the kind of writing you need to do. Draw a box around the Scoring Guide.

Many politicians and educators have suggested that students in public schools should wear school uniforms to make schools safer. Other people feel that uniforms keep students from expressing themselves freely.

Write an essay expressing your opinion on wearing school uniforms. Try to persuade your reader to adopt your point of view. Use facts and examples to support your reasons. Be sure your writing

- clearly states your opinion for your reader.

- is well organized. You should state a point of view, give a new reason in each paragraph, and restate your opinion.

- includes facts or examples to support each reason.

- leaves out confusing or unnecessary ideas so that reasons are sound and to the point.

- uses the conventions of language and spelling correctly.

your own writing Describe what the test asks you to do. Use your own words.

_____

_____

_____

_____

 Now go back to Ramon's work on page 246 in the Student Edition.

Prewriting

Gather and Organize

Choose a graphic organizer. Use it to organize my ideas.
Check my graphic organizer against the Scoring Guide.

Now it's time to practice these strategies. Go back and reread the writing prompt on page 122. Then fill in the persuasion map below to plan your persuasive essay about wearing school uniforms.

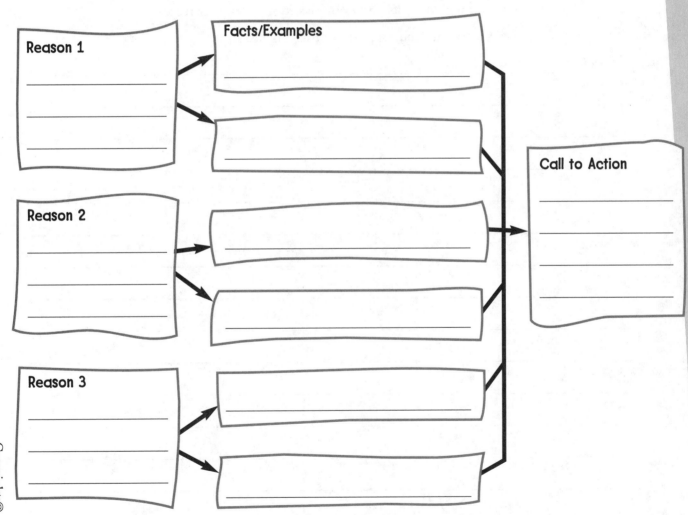

Now check your persuasion map against the Scoring Guide on page 122. Make any changes that you think will improve your persuasive essay.

 Now go back to Ramon's work on page 250 in the Student Edition.

Drafting

Write

Use my persuasion map to write a persuasive essay with reasons, facts, and examples.

your own writing

Now it's your turn to practice this strategy. Look back at the persuasion map you used to plan your persuasive essay about wearing school uniforms. Use your persuasion map to draft your persuasive essay. Make sure

- your opening paragraph clearly identifies the action you want readers to take.

- you include facts and examples to support your reasons.

- you restate your opinion in the conclusion.

_____

_____

_____

_____

_____

_____

_____

_____

_____

_____

_____

_____

_____

_____

_____

_____

_____

DRafting

Write
Use my persuasion map to write a persuasive essay with reasons, facts, and examples.

_____
_____
_____
_____
_____
_____
_____
_____
_____
_____
_____
_____
_____
_____
_____
_____
_____
_____

 Now go back to Ramon's work on page 252 in the Student Edition.

ReVising

Elaborate

Check what I have written against the Scoring Guide. Add any missing facts or examples.

Now it's your turn to practice this strategy. The paragraph below is part of one student's draft. The draft was written to persuade readers not to adopt school uniforms. Rewrite the paragraph. Add two or more facts or examples to support the reason that is the topic of this paragraph.

Some people have argued that having students wear uniforms makes schools safer. I think that is true in some places where there are gangs or where students are concerned about theft. However, here in Millville, kids already feel safe.

_____

_____

_____

_____

_____

_____

_____

_____

_____

_____

_____

_____

_____

_____

Remember: Use this strategy in **your own writing**

 Now go back to Ramon's work on page 253 in the Student Edition.

ReVising

Clarify

Check what I have written against the Scoring Guide. Make sure everything is clear.

Now it's your turn to practice this strategy. Read the paragraph below. (You will see some errors.) Draw a line through any parts that do not belong in the draft.

A second reason I oppose the idea of school uniforms has to do with letting kids express themself. I think it's fine to have some limits. Sure, some kids aren't appropriate choose clothes that arent really appropriate, like the following wearing midriff tops, wearing short shorts, or wearing their jeans too low. These are just a couple of styles that many kids like to wear. I hope you'll agree that a better way to fix these problems are by having a dress code not by requiring everyone to wear the same thing. Teenagers like to express who they are through their clothes and hair-styles. Listening to different kinds of music, choosing our friends, and joining clubs that interest us are other ways we show how we are unique. Forcing us all to dress a like makes us feel like clones.

Use the space below to explain your reasons for taking out any words above.

_____

_____

_____

_____

_____

_____

Remember: Use this strategy in **your own writing**

 Now go back to Ramon's work on page 254 in the Student Edition.

Editing

Proofread

Check that I have used correct grammar, capitalization, punctuation, and spelling.

⅃ Indent.   ℓ Take out something.
≡ Make a capital.   ⊙ Add a period.
/ Make a small letter.   ⌗ New paragraph
⋀ Add something.   SP Spelling error

Now it is time for you to practice this strategy. Below is a revised persuasive essay about wearing school uniforms. Use the proofreading marks to correct any errors in grammar, capitalization, punctuation, and spelling.

There has been some recent discussion about weather or not

students should be required to wear uniforms. requiring students

to wear uniforms would be a big mistake. I am very much

against it.

Some people has argued that having students wear uniforms

makes schools safer. I think that is true in some places where

their are gangs or where students are concerned about theft.

However, here in Millville, kids already feel safe No one makes a

big deal about what anyone is wearing. There is not a lot of

pressure too wear certain brand's or styles. I don't hardly know

of a single time that someone in our school was harmed because

of clothing except when my friend tripped on her shoelaces).

Why create problems where it don't exist?

⊐ Indent.

≡ Make a capital.

/ Make a small letter.

∧ Add something.

ℓ Take out something.

⊙ Add a period.

New paragraph

SP Spelling error

Editing

Proofread

Check that I have used correct grammar, capitalization, punctuation, and spelling.

A second reason I oppose the idea of school uniforms has to do with letting kids express themself. I think it's fine to have some limits. Sure, some kids choose clothes that arent really appropriate, like the following wearing midriff tops, wearing short shorts, or wearing their jeans too low. I hope you'll agree that a better way to fix these problems are by having a dress code not by requiring everyone to wear the same thing. Teenagers like to express who they are through their clothes and hairstyles. Forcing us all to dress a like makes us feel like clones. Me and my classmates are more likely to misbehave in school if we feel that our individuality is discouraged.

Lets forget about school uniforms for kids here in Millville and worry about some things that really matter.

Remember:
Use this strategy in
your own writing

RETURN Now go back to page 257 in the Student Edition.

Using a Rubric

This rubric for persuasive writing was made from the Scoring Guide on page 237 in the Student Edition.

Audience

How quickly and clearly is the writer's opinion presented to the audience?

Organization

How clearly and effectively has the writer organized the writing?

Elaboration

How effectively does the writer use facts and examples to support reasons for the opinion?

Clarification

How well does the writer avoid confusing or unnecessary ideas to make sure reasons are sound and to the point?

Conventions & Skills

How carefully does the writer follow conventions of language and spelling?

your own writing

Save this rubric. Use it to check your own writing.

Score 1 Point 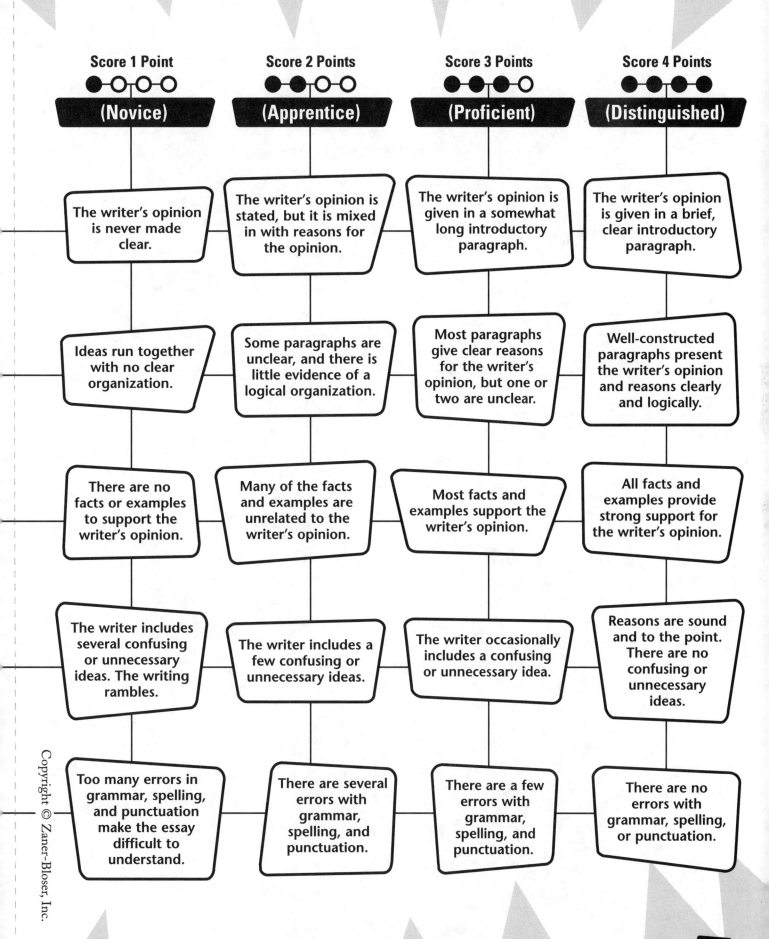	Score 2 Points	Score 3 Points	Score 4 Points
(Novice)	**(Apprentice)**	**(Proficient)**	**(Distinguished)**
The writer's opinion is never made clear.	The writer's opinion is stated, but it is mixed in with reasons for the opinion.	The writer's opinion is given in a somewhat long introductory paragraph.	The writer's opinion is given in a brief, clear introductory paragraph.
Ideas run together with no clear organization.	Some paragraphs are unclear, and there is little evidence of a logical organization.	Most paragraphs give clear reasons for the writer's opinion, but one or two are unclear.	Well-constructed paragraphs present the writer's opinion and reasons clearly and logically.
There are no facts or examples to support the writer's opinion.	Many of the facts and examples are unrelated to the writer's opinion.	Most facts and examples support the writer's opinion.	All facts and examples provide strong support for the writer's opinion.
The writer includes several confusing or unnecessary ideas. The writing rambles.	The writer includes a few confusing or unnecessary ideas.	The writer occasionally includes a confusing or unnecessary idea.	Reasons are sound and to the point. There are no confusing or unnecessary ideas.
Too many errors in grammar, spelling, and punctuation make the essay difficult to understand.	There are several errors with grammar, spelling, and punctuation.	There are a few errors with grammar, spelling, and punctuation.	There are no errors with grammar, spelling, or punctuation.